obsessions

collectors and their passions

obsessions

collectors and their passions

Stephen Calloway with Katherine Sorrell
Photography by Deidi von Schaewen

MITCHELL BEAZLEY

First published in 2004 by Mitchell Beazley,
an imprint of Octopus Publishing Group Ltd,
2–4 Heron Quays,
London E14 4JP

ISBN 1 84000 721 4

A CIP catalogue copy of this book is available
from the British Library

Commissioning Editor **Emma Clegg**
Executive Art Editor **Auberon Hedgecoe**
Senior Editors **Emily Anderson, Peter Taylor**
Designer **Emily Wilkinson**
Production Controller **Gary Hayes**
Copy-editor **Lindsay Porter**
Proofreader **Kim Richardson**
Indexer **Sandra Shotter**

Set in Meridien Roman and Rotis Serif

Printed and bound in China by
Toppan Printing Company Limited

CONTENTS

a little history of a great obsession

THE DESIRE TO COLLECT THINGS IS BY NO MEANS A UNIVERSAL ONE. HOWEVER, AMONG THOSE WHO ARE EITHER BLESSED OR AFFLICTED WITH THIS STRANGE COMPULSION, THE CONDITION IS ONE OF ALL-ENCOMPASSING FASCINATION. FOR THE TRUE COLLECTOR, THE PURSUIT AND ACQUISITION OF WORKS OF ART, BOOKS AND PRINTS, STAMPS OR SHOES OR SHELLS, EVEN PERHAPS OLD RADIO SETS, OBSOLETE PACKAGING, OR HUMBLE BUS TICKETS CAN BECOME A CONSUMING PASSION, THE BE-ALL AND END-ALL OF EXISTENCE.

Collecting is, of course, for most collectors just a reasonably absorbing and largely harmless pastime, looked upon by an uncomprehending world as a kind of gentle madness. For a few, however, it can become a dangerous preoccupation; its sensations – the breathless exhilaration of the quest, the thrill of capture, the enjoyment of the novelty, the sense of satisfaction and pride in possession – as addictive as the effects of any drug. But why do we collect? How did this passion to amass things become for so many a part of our collective psyche; what is the origin of this mysterious obsession?

Anthropologists have pointed to present-day collectors – pursuing, capturing, and displaying their treasures – as evidence of a survival into our own era of those great and once universal impulses of primitive existence which we enshrine in the notions of man the hunter-gatherer and woman the home-maker. Psychiatrists, treating collecting as a subject for examination – perhaps even as a disorder to be categorized as a form of mania – have suggested that some of mankind's most primitive conditionings and deep-seated competitive urges do indeed offer the best explanation of the phenomenon. Almost every species in nature has some idea of territory, but, with the possible exception of the thieving magpie or the bowerbird decking its love-nest with eye-catching trinkets, only the human race, it would appear, has a concept of possession and a desire to possess. Only man has framed the simple, brutal equation that in possessions lie status and power, or aspired to the more elevating ideal that "a thing of beauty is a joy forever".

The emergence of what we define as civilization is often considered to be indicated by the ability and desire to make and possess things that lie beyond the mere necessities of existence. From very early times, rulers have striven to amass treasure of different kinds and sought to possess objects imbued with magic or cult power. Some of these objects became numinous because they had been handed down from past generations or, having been taken as spoils of war, had become symbolic of triumph over enemies. We learn, for example, that in his palace Nebuchadnezzar II of Babylon preserved statues from the time of the Kings of Ur, even then many centuries old. This may be one of the first recorded cases of already ancient objects being venerated. Other exquisite Babylonian pieces, many now tragically scattered, suggest that here a new sensibility had begun to emerge.

LEFT **John Tradescant the Elder**, who had travelled as far as Russia and North Africa, formed one of the the greatest assemblage of natural curiosities of the 17th century. At his house, known as "Tradescant's Ark", his son continued to add to the collection.

PREVIOUS PAGE **In this imaginary cabinet** of curiosities by Johann Georg Heintz, dated 1666, the artist depicts a variety of natural objects including rare shells along with precious artifacts and jewels as an allegory of vanity.

The idea that objects might possess of themselves a value beyond their material and talismanic worth, an intrinsic value based simply upon their quality of design and exquisite workmanship – that is to say upon what we would call their beauty – marks a very great advance. The Egyptians seem to have understood something of this concept of beauty, but only with the rise of the early Greek civilizations in the Archaic period do we begin to sense that things are revered and desired entirely for their aesthetic worth. Sculptures cease to be just votive objects and become prized as things of beauty. Pictures begin to be painted as decorative objects in their own right and the decoration of pottery rises to new heights of sophistication. And almost for the first time these new kinds of beautiful objects are found not just in temples and public places, but in the private houses of those who could afford to collect them. The age of the work of art and of art collectors had arrived.

By the time of the Classical period in Greek civilization, and in particular during its high point in Athens in the 5th century BC, artists and craftsmen become known as individuals, their particular styles celebrated by an emerging circle of informed collectors. The appreciation of the works of sculptors in marble or bronze became ever-more sophisticated, whilst at much the same time a taste developed amongst connoisseurs for framed pictures and other small and easily portable works of art, including tiny figure sculptures, made from precious materials and intended to display cunning workmanship and to delight the hand and the eye. As collectors of such things became more numerous, the first merchants of works of art also appeared. With establishments in Athens and other great cities and also at the major ports such as Piraeus and Olbia, these early art-dealers carried on a lucrative trade that has, in its essentials, hardly changed to this day.

It is curious that whilst the Romans so comprehensively supplanted the Greeks in commercial power and, with military might, brought much of the known world under their sway, they lacked confidence in their own art. In spite of all its energy and delight in innovation and ostentation, for its ideals of beauty, its standards of craftsmanship, and for its very concept of visual and literary culture Rome still looked to Greece. For cultured Romans, Greek art seemed to belong to a lost Golden Age, all but impossible to replicate in a world in which artistic skills had irredeemably declined from their glorious state in Periclean Athens.

RIGHT Completed in 1631, the *Kunstschrank* of Gustavus Adolphus was made by the great cabinet-maker Hainhofer at Augsburg. The following year it was offered to the victorious king of Sweden as a bribe to spare the city, which lay in the path of his advancing armies.

NEXT PAGE One of a set of allegorical representations of the five senses, Jan Breughel's celebrated *Allegory of Sight* of 1617 shows an imaginary or ideal cabinet of extraordinary richness; however, many of the objects depicted, including paintings by Rubens and Breughel himself, are real and instantly recognizable.

Long before Rome's decadence, the taste for collecting ancient Greek sculpture and other works of art had already become a craze among the Roman aristocracy and intelligentsia. Philosophers and poets spoke of the nobility of the desire for beauty and patrician collectors considered their houses ennobled by antique pieces. The fall of Sicily – the richest of the Greek colonies – in the 3rd century BC gave a new impetus to the wholesale ransacking of older settlements for ancient marble and bronze statues. Roman merchants and powerful military commanders grew steadily more ruthless and collecting took on a more competitive edge. In 180 BC the victorious general Fulvius Nobilior paraded a vast collection of 785 bronze and 230 marble statues through the streets of Rome in a memorable triumph; these plundered works of art were eagerly fought over by collectors anxious to secure genuine pieces.

Caius Verres, Roman governor of Sicily around 73–71 BC, was so aggressive in his pursuit of statuary that Cicero said of this unspeakable rogue and bully that his "desire for art made him a robber and a criminal". How easily can the pursuit of beauty become mired in greed, unscrupulousness, madness, or even murder. By contrast, in the time of Julius Caesar, who found time to enjoy beautiful things and himself assembled an outstanding collection of intaglio gems and seals, we encounter many collectors and connoisseurs, whose refinement of taste would become legendary. Maecenas, a wealthy Roman knight and friend and benefactor of the poets Horace and Virgil, is the very type of the sophisticated art collector and has given his name to all such enlightened patrons.

Even at this date, art dealers played a devious game. To collectors with a good eye and a deep purse they supplied genuine Greek pieces or good later replicas of the originals made by the still highly skilled carvers of the Hellenistic period. For those who lacked either the funds or the discrimination to choose the best, there was a ready supply of recent and often wretchedly poor copies. A similar pattern would emerge when 18th-century English aristocrats visiting Rome on their Grand Tour sought to purchase real classical statues to send home to adorn the sculpture galleries of their neo-classical houses.

With the fall of Rome, Europe entered its Dark Ages. Whilst it is certainly the case that the idea of a total collapse of classical refinement has been overstated, it is nevertheless true that, in a

LEFT Typical of the spread of collecting beyond royal circles, the museum of Ferrante Imperato, the most prosperous pharmacist in Naples, was particularly rich in natural history specimens. In 1599 Imperato published a catalogue of his collection with this illustration of its principal room.

a little history of a great obsession

period lasting for several centuries, with barbarians at the gate, artistic and intellectual life struggled to hold on. Civilization survived at the courts of a few powerful rulers, but the Church alone became the repository of learning. In the chronicles of this savage age, we hear little of collecting and connoisseurship and much of the spoils of battle, of the gaudy ostentation of chieftains' halls and of the riches of their burial hoards. For several centuries, almost all domestic buildings – even royal residences – were utilitarian and primarily defensive. Beautiful objects were made, no doubt, but such things as gold drinking vessels, heavy jewellery, and ornate weaponry were considered treasure and were won and lost – and not infrequently simply melted down – according to the tides of fortune of ruthless warlords.

Throughout the ages, the powerful have always amassed treasure, loved luxury, and often commissioned the making of wonderful objects. Strangely though, the desire to own beautiful things simply because they are beautiful, to seek out the rare, to pursue art for art's sake – to be, in the sense that we use the word today, collectors – seems to be an impulse that really only revived during the 14th century. It first touched the early

Renaissance princely rulers of the great Italian cities, but then spread rapidly, almost as a craze, among their royal and noble cousins north of the Alps. Animated by a novel and genuine desire for learning and a new refinement of the senses, rulers increasingly began to withdraw from the ostentation of public court life and to seek out the contemplative peace of sequestered palace quarters where they could surround themselves with beautiful objects. The *studiolo* or cabinet, that perfect combination of private study, library, museum, and miniature art gallery, became the symbol of the new, precious sensibility of the cultivated prince.

At first these princely collectors made little distinction between the curiosities of nature and the work of painters and "cunning artificers". In sacrosanct apartments they gathered their most exquisite books alongside fossils and the skeletons of rare animals. The finest small pictures – or "cabinet works" – and pieces of sculpture could be found next to weirdly wrought timepieces; new-fangled globes mingled with coins, medals, and gems from the ancient world, as well as natural curiosities such as shells, precious corals, and other exotic objects brought back by travellers from distant oceans and new-found lands.

LEFT Andrea Odone, a rich Venetian merchant, chose to have himself portrayed in his portrait by Lorenzo Lotto of 1527 in the pose of a princely collector of classical sculpture, coins, medals, and other antiquities.

NEXT PAGE Successive generations of passionate collectors have added to the treasures of Burghley House near Stamford, creating a dense, layered effect that is typical of English country houses.

Such juxtapositions did not seem strange to these early collectors, and a privileged visitor in the 16th century admitted to view the Medici cabinets in Florence would not have been greatly surprised to find jumbled together in the same room the greatest of Cellini's busts of Duke Cosimo, a stuffed *cuccadrillo* (crocodile), a fine Greek amphora presented by a Venetian nobleman, and a so-called unicorn horn – in reality, of course, a narwhal's tusk – that had been one of old Piero de' Medici's favourite and most celebrated treasures.

In the North it became more customary for collections, in theory at least, to be segregated: *naturalia*, the wonders of the natural world, tended to arranged – often in complex patterns – in the cabinet of curiosities; pictures and sculptures were grouped in the *Kunstkammer* (cabinet of art), whilst the holy of holies, the *Schatzkammer*, an apartment more akin perhaps to the old treasury, enshrined objects prized for their fine or cunning workmanship and for the rarity and preciousness of their materials. In practice, however, these categories were far from rigorously observed; a good idea of the mix can be obtained from a close study of the detail in the many pictures that survive of both real and imaginary collector's hoards. Among the most extraordinary of these are the *Allegories of the Senses*, a set of paintings of idealized *Kunstkammern* by Jan "Velvet" Breughel that belonged originally to the Hapsburg Holy Roman Emperor Rudolf II, but which are now in the Prado in Madrid.

Rudolf was an intellectual and aesthetically minded prince, but also a brooding, melancholic man with a pronounced liking for exotic objects and erotic prints and pictures; in many ways he epitomizes the darker taste of the Mannerist era. In Prague, he presided over a weird court of astrologers, alchemists, necromancers, and pornographic artists; he allowed painters, printsellers, and curiosity dealers to display their wares in his great hall, whilst he filled his private cabinets with one of the greatest collections of rare and precious objects ever assembled. Arrayed with pictures by Giuseppe Arcimboldo, sculptures by Bartholomeus Spranger, and curious objects by the great goldsmith Wenzel Jamnitzer, his cabinets became the perfect expression of his idiosyncratic temperament and curious world-picture compounded of novel intellectual curiosity and old-fashioned superstition.

Becoming ever-more absorbed in his books and philosophical fantasies, Rudolf withdrew further from the perplexities of politics and, ultimately,

RIGHT Charles Towneley was one of the most obsessive 18th-century collectors of classical sculpture, which filled every corner of his London mansion. Johann Zoffany's painting of 1790 shows Towneley and his friends in the library of the house in Park Street.

in 1611, he was supplanted by his tougher and more worldly brother Matthias. This callous act of usurpation curiously echoes the fate of Prospero, the wronged duke and magician in *The Tempest*, Shakespeare's political fairy-tale first performed that very year. Tragically, Rudolf died the following year, still believing that, like Prospero he would be allowed to keep his books and that his superb collections would be his monument; in the event, during the last days of the Thirty Years War all fell prey to the troops of the avaricious Queen Christina of Sweden, who had long desired to possess the Emperor's pictures and other treasures. Rudolf's cabinets were sacked, and his vast library – the books brutally stripped of their covers to lighten the load – piled onto more than a hundred wagons for the long journey North.

Throughout the 16th and 17th centuries, the great heyday of the *Kunstkammern*, collecting was undertaken upon the most lavish scale. Princes exchanged the most costly of gifts. They emptied their treasuries in pursuit of rare items such as carved rhinoceros horns and examples of true porcelain from the East, and they competed – often ruthlessly – to secure the services of the best artists, such as Leonardo da Vinci or Benvenuto Cellini.

Although the creation of *Kunstkammern* still remained almost exclusively the preserve of princes and the great nobles in the earlier decades, as the 17th century progressed collecting became more widespread. Successful artists such as Rubens, whose house in Antwerp resembled a small palace, displayed their wealth and taste by accumulating old and contemporary pictures, drawings, prints, and pieces of classical statuary. Not surprisingly, many of the most celebrated cabinets of natural curiosities were the creations of scholars, travellers, and merchants. Several, such those of Ferrante Imperato of Naples (founded in 1599), of Francesco Calceolari the apothecary of Verona, and the private museum of Olaus Worm of Copenhagen, are known from delightful illustrations in their respective catalogues.

In London, as early as 1628, the Tradescants, a father and son both named John, formed one of the most intriguing cabinets of curiosities, which they called The Ark, in a house in Lambeth. By no means the only English collection of its kind, it was certainly one of the most varied and extensive. John Tradescant the Younger published a catalogue in 1656 and also, for posterity, had himself painted with a heap of his most prized exotic shells. Later the Tradescant treasures passed

LEFT **The Regency architect Sir John Soane formed one of the most extraordinary collections of architectural fragments, plaster casts, and other curiosities, massing his treasures in three adjacent terraced houses in London's Lincoln's Inn Fields.**

into the hands of the antiquary Elias Ashmole, and as a result many are preserved still in the "Founder's Collection" that forms the nucleus of the Ashmolean Museum in Oxford.

One of the last great princes in the old *Kunstkammer* tradition, Augustus the Strong, Elector of Saxony and King of Poland, was one of the most ardent of all collectors. His love of beautiful women, his passion for building, expressed in the palaces of Dresden, and his lust for oriental ceramics, which led to the discovery by Hans Böttger of the secret of true porcelain and the establishment of the Meissen factory, have all become the stuff of legend. Augustus's obsession with organizing his collections into different categories in separate locations (a paintings gallery and print cabinet, an armoury, porcelain in a "Japanese Palace", and so forth) led to an unprecedented degree of systemization, and – extraordinarily at the time – to his opening his treasure chamber, the Green Vault, and other parts of the collection to the public. Ironically, this has been seen in some ways to herald the dawning of a new democratic museum age and to signal the beginning of the end of the essentially private, princely cabinet.

Of course, many of the great assemblages of *Kunstkammer* treasures, such as those in the Residenz palace in Munich, in the Dresden Green Vault, or those of the Medici in the Museo degli Argenti in Florence, have been carefully preserved. But to a great extent, through the intervention of 19th- and 20th-century curatorial ideals, the essential flavour of the older collections has all too often been diluted or entirely lost. It is in quieter backwaters, in the Alpine castle of Ambras, which houses Ferdinand of Tyrol's eccentric collections, or in the dark and dusty closets of Rosenborg Castle, the old royal residence in Copenhagen, that we can sniff something of the true atmosphere of the old cabinets of curiosities.

Today, in museums we can see exquisite and amazing objects of all kinds and from every culture, but these exhibits have inevitably become divorced, for the most part, from the passionate feelings of their previous owners. It is now perhaps only in the houses of private collectors that we can still sense the compulsions which drove the great aesthetes and connoisseurs of past ages. Only in the presence of collectors themselves can we hope to understand the indefatigability in the pursuit of beauty, the overwhelming intensity of desire, and that exultant joy in possession that have across the centuries constituted the true collector's obsessions.

RIGHT Napoleon's megalomaniac vision of massing Europe's greatest art treasures in a public gallery at the Louvre ushered in a new era of museum collecting. Zix's allegorical portrait depicts Napoleon's art-expert and curator Vivant Denon arranging the loot of his campaigns.

grand old traditional

NOTHING IS MORE FAITHFUL TO THE HISTORY OF COLLECTING THAN THE GRAND ACCUMULATION OF HISTORICAL ART AND ARTEFACTS. SOMETIMES VALUABLE, OFTEN LARGE SCALE, AND ALWAYS IMPRESSIVE, SUCH PIECES MAY HAVE BEEN HANDED DOWN THROUGH GENERATIONS OF THE SAME FAMILY, OR TRACKED DOWN AND PUT TOGETHER WITH UNSTINTING PERSEVERANCE AND DEDICATION BY TODAY'S KNOWLEDGEABLE OWNERS.

"What joy these old things are to live with, each piece made by the hand of a craftsman".

Charles Paget Wade, Snowshill, Glos, England
ARTEFACTS

Charles Paget Wade was an unconventional collector. His rule was simple: if an object showed a high degree of craftsmanship, design, or colour then, to him, it was worthy of acquiring; just as worthy as any object deemed conventionally to be high art. Thus, in his collection, gathered from his childhood in the late 19th century until his death in 1956, there exist side by side butter stamps, cow bells, bicycles, musical instruments, clocks, toys, spinning wheels, and looms; objects of utility but also, to Wade, of beauty and distinction.

Wade's joy in such objects was fostered early on. Sent to stay at the age of seven with his grandmother in Great Yarmouth, Norfolk, so he could attend a local school, he was left very much to his own devices. Though solitary, he was happy, enjoying exploring the seashore, watching Punch and Judy shows, day-dreaming and, most of all, viewing – once a week only – the contents of Granny Spencer's Chinese cabinet, which was filled with a selection of tiny, fascinating objects. A bone model of a spinning jenny, a Christmas tree angel with golden wings, and a pair of musical boxes were typical. Wade was inspired to become a collector himself, and began to buy small curios from his pocket money.

Having gained little from school but an aptitude for drawing and wood-work, Wade set out to become an architect, and eventually secured a job with Parker & Unwin, a firm that was then one of the leading exponents of the Arts and Crafts movement. Four years later, however, the death of Wade's father gave him a private income from the family's sugar estates in St Kitts, and Wade, having no need to work, left his job and concentrated instead on book illustration.

During World War I, Wade served in the Royal Engineers. Even in the midst of the devastation of the Western Front, he hung his room with pictures, put up shelves, and found an attractive cover for his bunk. He read back copies of *Country Life* magazine for diversion and, looking for a manor house in which to house his collection, one day he came across an advert for Snowshill Manor in the property pages. When the war was over, the house was still on the market, and in 1919 Wade decided to buy it.

A typical English Cotswold manor house, with parts dating back to 1500, Snowshill was, by the time of Wade's purchase, semi-derelict, its garden a jungle.

ABOVE A Cantonese shrine cabinet from the Grey Room. It dates from the 1700s and shows European influence in the detailing.

RIGHT An array of instruments, including cellos, hurdy-gurdies, oboes, clarinets, flutes, bassoons, and bugles are gathered in the Music Room.

With the help of 28 men, Wade completely restored the property, aiming to recapture its historical atmosphere. By this time, he had already been collecting for 20 years or so, and he began to fill the house with his finds. He had very particular ideas about display – a sense of mystery was important, for instance, and the Manor's interiors were designed so as to mystify, surprise, and provoke the beholder's imagination. A sense of drama played a large part in all this, and the lighting was carefully designed to enhance the objects, while each room was arranged so that everything within it was harmonious, with subtle backdrops of paint and panelling allowing the viewer to study the collections without distraction. Often, the addition of a new object meant that an entire room

had to be rearranged. Not only that, but Wade himself sometimes added to the dramatic atmosphere by appearing from a dark corner or a secret passage, dressed in an antique costume. Meanwhile, Wade continued to travel all over England on hunting trips, returning with neglected discoveries of all kinds, to be restored at Snowshill's workshops and placed in appropriate settings.

At first, Wade collected mainly English household objects. But he loved colour, and eventually began to collect European painted furniture and Far Eastern crafts, with which he created stunning tableaux. Amazingly, though, almost everything was collected in Britain. The Japanese armour, for example, was found in Cheshire, in a plumber's shop in

ABOVE The Green Room contains a remarkable collection of 26 suits of Japanese samurai armour of the 17th–19th centuries. Wade acquired them between 1940 and 1945 from various parts of England, and arranged them to create the impression of a company of warriors meeting in the gloom.

Cheltenham and in a cellar off London's Charing Cross Road. Wade was always curious about an object's workings, about who had made it and how, about what it was used for, and who by. "I have not bought things because they were rare or valuable," he said. "There are many things of everyday use in the past, of small value, but of interest as records of various vanished handicrafts. What joy these old things are to live with, each piece made by the hand of a craftsman; each has a feeling and individuality that no machine could ever attain."

Ironically, Wade never actually lived at Snowshill. It was reserved for his collection and for entertaining (visitors included John Betjeman, Virginia Woolf, Clough Williams-Ellis, Graham Greene, and JB Priestley), while he made his home at the one-bedroom cottage, known as the Priest's House, next door. A modest home without electricity, this, too, was filled with a multitude of objects.

In 1946, Wade married and subsequently spent much of his time in the West Indies, though he always remained greatly interested in Snowshill and continued to add to the collection. In 1951 he presented the house, and its 20,000-strong collection, to the National Trust, which continues to run the Manor. Wade died in 1956, having just bought a set of Sicilian carriage carvings – a collector to the very last. As Jonathan Howard, Snowshill's steward, says: "He was a maximalist. He loved what these objects provoked. They were friends to him."

"There wasn't much to do except wander round the hills, and that's when I started collecting."

Bob Edgar, Old Trail Town, Cody, WY, USA

WILD WEST

In the Wild West few places were more lawless than the frontier towns of Wyoming. Take the bloodthirsty tale of Belle Drury, for example. Tried but acquitted of the murder of her boyfriend, the noted outlaw William Gallagher, dance hall girl Drury led a rackety life in the town of Arland where, during a wild party in her cabin one night, a man called Jesse Conway so provoked her that she grabbed a gun and shot him dead. This was one step too far and, later that night, Drury herself was murdered in retaliation: a brutal end to what was a short, turbulent, and violent life.

Or take the story of John Johnston. A giant of a man at six foot six, Johnston was born in New Jersey in 1824. He went West in the early 1840s as a trapper and worked his way to the Yellowstone region, where he married a Flathead Indian woman. They lived happily until his wife and unborn child were killed and gruesomely mutilated by Crow Indians. So began a 12-year search for revenge, in which Johnston was said sometimes to cut out and eat the liver of an enemy he had killed, earning him the nickname Liver-eating Johnston. Subsequently, Johnston fought in the Civil War, ran a wood yard, became Chief of Scouts for General Nelson A Miles, was made a marshal and then a sheriff, and died at the ripe old age of 76 in 1900.

The lives of both Drury and Johnston, as well as others, including Jim White the Buffalo Hunter and Phillip Vitter, a trapper killed by a grizzly bear, are immortalized at Old Trail Town, a museum of the Old West in Cody, Wyoming, created by archaeologist, historian, and artist Bob Edgar and his wife Terry. Its main feature is a collection of 26 frontier buildings, dating from 1879–1901, which have been acquired from the north-west Wyoming area and painstakingly reconstructed, then filled with historical relics to give a faithful flavour of the frontier era. There are cabins belonging to a trapper, a hunter, and an Indian scout, a saloon (with bullet holes still visible in the door), two blacksmith's, a carpenter's shop, post office, school, and a couple of general stores, as well as a hideout used by Butch Cassidy and the Sundance Kid and their infamous Hole in the Wall gang. The old wagon tracks still run in front of the Old Trail Town buildings, and nearby is a cemetery where our colourful characters are

RIGHT **With patience and determination, Bob Edgar set about acquiring the cabins that make up Old Trail Town, first persuading their owners to part with them, then painstakingly numbering each log, dismantling them, and transporting them back to Cody, Wyoming, in order to reassemble them and fill them with historical relics.**

buried. To complete the picture there are wagons, carts, buggies, a stagecoach, and a hearse, guns, clothing, and a host of other items of memorabilia, as well as a Museum of the Old West, which houses prehistoric and historic Plains Indian artefacts.

Bob Edgar grew up in northern Wyoming, and spent his childhood roaming around the ranches and exploring the hidden coves of the Big Horn Basin. "There wasn't much to do except wander around the hills, and that's when I first started collecting artefacts – arrowheads, old tools, a lost bottle," he says. "I started noticing that little by little a lot of these old abandoned cabins out on the range were either falling in or being destroyed by grazing cattle. Some were even being sawed up for firewood. I thought somebody should save them, but nobody was doing anything about it."

Eventually, Bob decided to make it his mission to preserve these relics of days gone by. In

1965 he and Terry married and bought five acres of land on the site where Buffalo Bill and his associates had surveyed the first town site of Cody City in 1895. Along with it they acquired a log cabin dating from the 1890s that had been used as a trading post.

In the spring of 1967 they set up home in the one-room cabin, hauling water and using a wood stove, and set about collecting what was necessary to realize their dream. "Everywhere we went I'd talk to people about what we were trying to do," says Edgar. "If they had an interesting old cabin I'd offer to buy it or try to persuade them to donate it to us to preserve it. Some would, others wouldn't. Many would say maybe later." Sometimes it took years, but once a cabin had been acquired, Edgar would go to the site, number the logs, make drawings of the structure, and then dismantle and transport it back to Cody. Here, he would reassemble it on new foundations, renovating

as necessary. And so, little by little, Old Trail Town came into being.

If guts, determination, and sheer stubbornness were among the more admirable qualities of the original inhabitants of the frontier towns, Edgar has shown that he is a true descendant. Without much money or any commercial support – but armed with enormous drive and determination – he has created an authentic, original, and personal vision. The boardwalks of Old Trail Town may now be empty, the cabins no longer inhabited and the wagons unridden, but close your eyes and draw in a deep breath and it is possible to picture the smoke rising from the trapper's chimney once again, and to hear the piano in the saloon bar or the horses panting as they draw up outside the post office. A ghost town this may be, but it is far from being dead: the extraordinary people, places, and events of the Wild West are still living and breathing in this remarkable collection.

ABOVE AND LEFT Edgar has gone to great lengths to furnish the homes, stores, and other cabins of Old Trail Town with authentic relics of the past. One of the two general stores contains the type of provisions, from food to clothing, that the inhabitants of the West were able to buy.

"Everyone makes mistakes, but if you enjoy yourself, even the mistakes are nice mistakes."

Ernst von Loesch, Berlin, Germany
ARCHITECTURAL DESIGN

There is a pleasing unity about Ernst von Loesch's different collections. In colour, material, shape, and size, they complement each other marvellously. First, there are the architectural drawings – two-dimensional, rectangular, relatively monochromatic, a nice combination of the reasoned and the imagined. Then there are the architectural models – three-dimensional, in elegant marble, fine cork, or subtle bronze, generally classic but sometimes showing livelier Baroque tendencies. There are, too, some wonderful drawings by well-known Impressionist artists. That these sophisticated pieces are occasionally juxtaposed with eccentric finds, such as an antique lottery machine or a strange device for spinning wool, for example, just goes to show that von Loesch is not only concerned with mellow good taste, but likes to throw in the odd surprise here and there as well.

Von Loesch's eye, with its clever mix of connoisseurship and curiosities, was developed in his former career as a successful interior decorator. He spent 20 years planning and drawing, and often arranged clients' collections for them. At the same time, he owned an antiques shop, selling the usual furniture, glass, mirrors, porcelain, and so on; but when, 15 years or so ago, recession hit the decorating industry, he decided to shift careers. The decision was straightforward: he had for several years been collecting architectural drawings of the 18th and 19th centuries for his own pleasure; through this, and his work, he had built up some expertise, and he decided to go into business as a dealer, thus creating an ideal combination of work and pleasure. And so, von Loesch made an office in the corner of his Berlin apartment, and his collection – or parts of it, at least – became his profession. Which means that von Loesch is in the enviable position of watching his collection change, little by little, over the course of years, as he sells and acquires different pieces.

There are some things he will never sell, however. These include the first two drawings he ever bought: one a French competition work by a student at the Ecole des Beaux-Arts, dating from around 1830, and showing a building similar to the Pantheon, the other a southern Bavarian work of around 1750, depicting an elaborate Baroque church. They are both very high quality, but their

RIGHT **On a beautiful German Baroque chest stand von Loesch's nativity-scene model horse, 19th-century lottery machine, and an iron tool for spinning wool. On the wall behind are drawings by Impressionist painters.**

ABOVE In von Loesch's office architectural drawings are hung on the walls, while models stand on bookshelves and on the floor. In the centre is a German chapel of unknown provenance, while in the foreground is a large model of one of the first neo-Gothic churches in Germany.

monetary value is not what matters to von Loesch: "Some drawings I just like very much, they mean a lot to me and I keep them whether they are valuable or not. It is sentimental, but I suppose I am more of a collector than I am a dealer." The pair of drawings clearly demonstrates what it is that von Loesch so loves about this genre. On the one hand the French design represents the cool and classical; on the other, the Bavarian symbolizes the florid and Baroque. "I'm attracted to the mix between the decorative nature of the drawings and the fact that they also show detailed engineering," he explains. "It's a combination of the nice-looking and the dry. They work together so well, and that's what appeals to me."

One of the few dealers in this esoteric area, von Loesch generally has about 400 drawings at any one time, ranging from the very simple to the very

fine. All were drawn in either pen and ink or, less frequently, chalk, and they spring from one of three sources: studies carried out by students of architecture; drawings of famous monuments, measured and planned out but sometimes embellished, by travelling architects; and working drawings for their own projects by practising architects of the time. Ironically, of the latter it is generally the drawings of never-realized schemes that come onto the market, as those that were actually built were usually kept by their owners. Because of this, von Loesch is particularly proud to possess a sketch by the renowned British classical architect Robert Adam for the country house Luton Hoo.

About ten years ago, on the advice of a friend, von Loesch began to complement his drawing collection with small-scale models. "Not everyone

understands about the drawings," he explains. "You have got to have the mind for it. But, with models, even someone who isn't very interested in architecture can appreciate them." He was lucky enough to start off with several good examples that he found at major auctions in London, and began to build up this collection, too. The models, almost all made as souvenirs of the Grand Tour of the 18th and 19th centuries, range from Roman columns to churches, coliseums to obelisks, bridges to staircases, and arches to monuments, and go from just a few centimetres in size to more than a metre. As von Loesch became well known for his collecting and dealing, so other dealers began to seek him out and offer him choice examples, and so it went on. He now has the biggest collection of these models in Germany, comprising somewhere between 60 and 80 in number, including

about 20 very impressive (and unusual) three-dimensional cork pictures.

And then came the curiosities. As every good decorator knows, you have to have something a little different with which to offset acres of good taste, and von Loesch has some unusual pieces. He veers a little towards the playful – he loves the mid 19th-century lottery machine with its spherical cage and wooden handle, and also a rather attractive, posing horse, once part of an Austrian nativity scene of about 1800. And what about the bizarre, spindly contraption that spins wool, the miniature tomb of Napoleon, or the inkwell topped by a winged lion? "Oh yes, it should be a little bit peculiar," he avers. "When you are a collector you must enjoy yourself. Everyone makes mistakes, but if you enjoy yourself, even the mistakes are nice mistakes."

ABOVE Typical of the collection is an arrangement of obelisks in marble and bronze. The picture on the right is a sketch of a Roman temple to Vesta.

*"I have always wanted to live in the past –
whatever my passion, I have to live in it."*

Lillian Williams, Normandy & Provence, France
18TH-CENTURY ARTEFACTS

Once upon a time there was a young woman called Lillian Williams who simply adored the opera. She used to attend performances in 18th-century costume, attended by a footman and, sometimes, in a sedan chair carried by lackeys or in a coach pulled by horses. Now this was quite unusual, for it was 20th-century San Francisco – not that our heroine worried.

As the years passed, she was married – to a like-minded man who collected antique keyboard instruments – and the fairytale continued, only now Williams and her husband had moved to France. She decorated their properties in authentic 18th-century style, with no more than one lightbulb per room (if any), and all the accoutrements of 18th-century life scattered around, as if the characters of *Les Liaisons Dangereux* – her favourite novel – had just this minute got up and left.

"In the 18th century everything was so beautiful, from the most modest object upwards. Everything had a spirit of tranquillity," declares Williams. "I was brought up in the isolated American West, but I really think I was born with these instincts. I have always wanted to live in the past – whatever my passion, I have to live in the middle of it. I take great exception to the ways of the 21st century. Beauty is not the modality today at all." Williams collects compulsively anything to do with 18th-century life, up to the French Revolution and not a minute after, including furniture, paintings, textiles, accessories, and costumes. The items come mostly from France and were acquired, over the years, from a variety of sources, such as flea markets, auctions, shops, and country sales. Accessories and costumes are Williams' pride and joy because, though she loves the whole of the 18th century, her greatest passion is for the things that really speak of history, the secret, private things that surprise by having survived for more than 200 years. "There's just nothing more ephemeral or closer to the 18th century than what people wore," she says. Williams' costume collection is probably unrivalled, and indeed much of it is already on loan to museums. She also collects ephemera – brushes, combs, powder boxes, ribbons, stockings, and, in particular, pieces made from card, paper, or papier-mâché, including a clock, two portraits on cardboard of Louis XV, and a paper hat from the Castle Howard Collection. "I love things that are lost and broken," says Williams.

RIGHT Lillian Williams bought the beautiful 18th-century Venetian mannequin from a dealer in Florence. Every piece of clothing is authentic, from her corset to her silk stockings.

ABOVE This room in the Williams' Normandy house is filled with porcelain that was excavated years ago by Ted Williams from the cellar of their apartment in Paris. He painstakingly glued it all together, forming one of their first collections. Lillian Williams hand-painted the walls of the room with motifs taken from the china.

RIGHT In the Williams' house in Provence, Ted uses this attic room as his office, where he is surrounded by the accoutrements of the 18th century. "The room as a whole didn't have much going for it, so I tented it with Laura Ashley fabric," says Lillian Williams.

She and her husband, Ted, do a great deal of research and restoration, though Williams does not believe in over-restoring: "Things shouldn't look like new," she asserts, "they should look like old. And they should only be restored when in extreme peril." The pair are, of course, incredibly knowledgeable about their period, though Williams says she feels that the best knowledge comes from instinct, and while it's possible to spend a great deal of money, one can also create fabulous effects from imagination and illusion. For her, collecting is all about theatre and ego. Every room in each of her houses is a stage set, arranged in the best possible way to create the ambience of the 18th century. In other words, though she may have a number of, say, hand-painted snuff boxes, she will not display them

together, but will dot one or two around a room as they would have been used. "My collection is arranged as my environment," she explains. But do they really live like that, all the time? The answer is yes... and no. They sleep on 18th-century beds, the mattresses stuffed with wool from sheep kept at their Normandy house, but they don't always sit on the straight-back 18th- century chairs, despite having about 500 of them. They have limited the use of electricity, much preferring candles. "We don't wear 18th-century costumes every day either," laughs Williams, adding: "Though we'd like to. And we have telephones and videos – but we sure as hell don't have the Internet." Some concessions to modernity, it seems, are just going too far.

ABOVE Ted Williams has a collection of about 40 antique keyboard instruments, many of them painted. Some have been restored so they can be played. Lillian Williams hand-painted the walls of this room, too.

"We don't consider the collection macabre, but it probably is a peek into our macabre side."

Rick Ellis & Thomas Jayne, New York, NY, USA
NATURAL HISTORY

When a celebrated food stylist and a renowned interior designer share a 140 sq m (1,500 sq ft) New York loft, you expect the results to be admirable. Add in a pair of intriguing yet complementary collections as well, however, and you have the perfect recipe for a truly impressive home.

Rick Ellis is a culinary historian as well as being a leading food stylist (he designed the food for Martin Scorsese's film *The Age of Innocence*, among others) and his collection consists of a library of around 5,000 books – recipe books and volumes relating to the history of American food and the practice of cooking, dating back to the late 1700s. Thomas Jayne trained in architecture and art history, and is regularly ranked as one of America's top decorators. His collection encompasses the decorative arts, sculpture (especially the work of Houdon), and his books related to Mediterranean gardening. And the pair have a shared interest in natural history specimens (human and animal skulls, antlers, and seashells), engravings and, as they modestly put it, a painting or two. Both men are, it goes without saying, experts in their fields, extremely knowledgeable and with a great eye.

Ellis began his collection while at college ("I needed to feed myself," he explains) and, as his interest in the subject grew, so did his library. He bought, occasionally to start with, mid 20th-century American cookbooks from flea markets and the like, and by the time he and Jayne met he had acquired about 100 books. Jayne, who had just finished graduate school with a degree in early American culture, encouraged him to collect more determinedly, and a goal emerged to have a representative collection of American cookbooks. This Ellis has undeniably achieved, having amassed a collection *par excellence*, in which his favourite titles are a first edition of *The Joy of Cooking*, and a 1787 copy of *American Cookery*, the first cookbook written by an American. Jayne, meanwhile, had always been interested in the idea of cabinets of curiosity, and the pair began to assemble their collection of antiques, stuffed animals, mounted antlers, and so on. Eventually, they started to buy *memento mori*, too – objects such as skulls and skeletons that serve to remind us of our own mortality – as and when

RIGHT In Ellis and Jayne's elegant New York loft, more than 5,000 American cookbooks are kept on specially designed shelves, acting both as a display and a convenient reference for Ellis, a renowned food stylist and culinary historian.

they came across them. "We don't consider the collection macabre as such," says Ellis, "but it probably is a peek into our macabre side."

Although, over the years, they have not exactly been obsessive collectors, they have been determined and, just occasionally, swept away by their unruly passion. Ellis remembers one of their first major natural history purchases – an antelope skull bought more than 25 years ago for $125, which seemed to him then an ungodly amount to spend on something so frivolous. They have bought pieces on their travels – a large painting purchased in London, for example, cost more to ship back to the US than it did to buy – and they have travelled in order to buy. Ellis once flew to Paris for the auction of a

remarkable cookbook collection, with the intent just to look at the books. But the one book he wanted – and eventually got – was immediately pre-empted by the French government.

Today, Ellis's books are kept in enormous bookcases which were specially designed for their loft, creating a considered display and also a handy and easy-to-access reference for his day-to-day work. The other pieces are arranged on any available shelves, window ledges, and flat surfaces, in an order that owes more to visual effect than any pedantic system of age, type, or provenance. And that effect is, of course, just as it ought to be: deft and apparently casual – at once thoroughly enjoyable and unselfconsciously attractive.

ABOVE *Memento mori* and natural history specimens are displayed on any available flat surfaces. Objects are arranged aesthetically rather than logically, with colour and texture overriding a more scholarly approach.

LEFT As well as cookbooks, Ellis and Jayne have collected antique furniture, natural history specimens, *memento mori*, decorative objects, sculpture, engravings, and paintings. The large painting shown here is one of their favourite pieces.

"My house is a landmark. But it's not for everyone. All my collecting led to this."

Hunt Slonem, Kingston, NY, USA
NEO-GOTHIC FURNITURE

When you knock at the door of Hunt Slonem's house in Kingston, in Upstate New York, you half expect it to open with a slow creak and to be met by an ageing, mad-eyed butler and a dismembered hand scuttling across the hallway. For Slonem's stately home was considered as a location for the *Addams Family* movie (though the film-makers' overtures were turned down by the house's previous owners), and as a Gothic mansion with the full works of horror movie ingredients – barring the dust, cobwebs, and actual monsters – it can't be beaten.

The house, called The Cordts Mansion, was built in 1873, part of an estate overlooking the Hudson River, and comes with 13 acres of land, stables, and five gazebos. It has a not-inconsequential 30 rooms, including ten bedrooms. The house was built to look at Kingston Point, with grounds designed by Frederick Law Olmsted, who laid out New York's Central Park. It is very much an intact, well-preserved, Second Empire property, and Slonem has filled it with his eminent and unique collection of American neo-Gothic furniture (including an extraordinary 150 chairs), every piece of which is consistent with the period of the house, give or take a decade.

Originally a medieval style, Gothic became fashionable again in England in the late 18th century, sparked by the building of Strawberry Hill, Horace Walpole's impressive little Gothic castle in Surrey, and assisted by King George IV's decision to redesign Windsor Castle in the Gothic style. For almost a century, Gothic was popular in England, spreading to Europe and then the newly independent United States of America by the mid 1800s, where it lent an air of tradition and history to the young nation and became a status symbol for wealthy homeowners. Features included perpendicular lines, pointed arches, and deep mouldings, used for the design of both furniture and entire houses.

Until recently, Slonem's passion for Victorian furniture ("I've always loved the old and creepy," he says) was decidedly outré. "It was terribly unpopular," he says. "In the 1950s and '60s, especially, they used the furniture for firewood." Thanks in part to the Houston Museum of Fine Arts' exhibition, *The Gothic Taste in America*, in 1976, it has now become quite fashionable to collect

RIGHT In one of many drawing rooms in Slonem's stately home a magnificent cast iron mantelpiece is displayed. It is original to the property and is one of only four such in the country. The clock, candelabra, and table are all neo-Gothic.

ABOVE Above a neo-Gothic cabinet hangs one of Slonem's paintings, a portrait of his friend the Countess Oberenevitch. The chairs are English, perhaps by Augustus Pugin, though they are not actually Gothic.

Victoriana – though it still isn't everybody's favourite. "Oh, my house is a landmark," says Slonem. "But it's not for everyone." Which came first, the house or the collection? The collection, by many years – and buying the house was part of an inevitable progression. "All my collecting led to this," he says.

Described as "an insatiable shopper", Slonem buys his pieces from flea markets, which he attends constantly, and auctions, particularly sales in the South, where there are still some great buys to be had. Like most serious collectors, he adores the thrill of the chase. "It's so exciting, I practically faint when I'm bidding on something. It's like a horse-race, or a drug." He started collecting, he says, because neo-Gothic was affordable, available, and distinctive. Now he can't stop, though he points out that he is an

inveterate collector of other things, too. As well as the furniture, he has about 50 Gothic revival perfume bottles, a collection second only in size to that of Lee Anderson, his friend and mentor (see page 58). He also collects shells, moths, and butterflies, the latter in the form of antique specimens which have been painstakingly re-catalogued and hung in museum-quality cases. Not so long ago he put together a collection of beautiful glass by Blenko, America's oldest makers of hand-blown glass, in about a month. He has collected witches' balls, chandeliers, 19th-century American picture frames, fish, plants (he is an avid gardener) and, last, but by no means least, live birds, about 100 of them at present, including hornbills, toucans, finches, and a friendly yellowhead Amazon parrot called Oliver.

Slonem is a renowned artist, whose large works, often crowded with birds, can be seen in more than 70 museums around the world, including the Guggenheim and the Metropolitan Museum in New York. His paintings are bold, colourful, and distinctly untraditional, yet he traces a clear link between them and his radically different home surroundings. "There's a tradition of painting this subject matter – the natural world – here on the Hudson."

Slonem has certainly not been afraid to use colour in his home, where deep tones on the walls provide a backdrop for the striking, confident shapes of his chairs, sofas, ottomans, sideboards, mantels, and other intriguing pieces. His current favourite is a recently acquired sofa that was designed for a Louisiana plantation house. It is one of a pair, and its

mate is in the Met in New York. He is also "crazy" about his perfume bottles, and adores his three Jones chairs. They came from the Jones-Schimmerhan house on the Hudson, where the phrase "keeping up with the Joneses" originated. "Most of it is just what I like, though," he says. "I don't care about its value. I have a good eye and I sort of collect by osmosis."

The collection is not so much displayed as arranged, in a suitably colour-coordinated fashion (rich reds predominating), for this is a living, breathing home, and Slonem uses every square inch of it, whether for work, giving parties, or hosting more formal gatherings. He sits on his sofas, puts drinks on his sideboards and leans on his mantelpieces. The look may be 19th century, but it is part of a very 21st-century lifestyle.

ABOVE Another drawing room, painted a dramatic black, is furnished with distinctively well-upholstered Victorian pieces. The rabbit paintings are by Slonem, and are in Victorian Eastlake frames.

"The ability to empathize with other eras and situations is an important human quality."

Georg Laue, Munich, Germany
CURIOSITIES

The world of Georg Laue is one of wonders, miracles, and curiosities. In 21st-century Munich he has assembled a collection worthy of a Renaissance prince, a collection of unique treasures, mostly from the 16th and 17th centuries, to amaze and delight our modern sensibilities.

A dealer, historian, and publisher as well as a collector, Laue established his business, the Kunstkammer Georg Laue, in 1997, in the heart of Munich's gallery district. What is a *Kunstkammer*? It is, literally, a cabinet of curiosities or – known as a *Wunderkammer* – a chamber of wonders, in the tradition of the chambers that were created alongside royal treasuries in the early 16th century. Encyclopaedic collections that reflected the admiration of all that was exotic and beautiful in nature, art, and technology, they also demonstrated an interest in the new systematic ordering of things. The classification and display of *Kunstkammer* objects, in fact, helped lead to the development of the earliest museums. And *Kunstkammer* collectors were enthusiastic, wealthy, and determined – their finds might start in a cabinet, but would then overflow into hall after hall, and eventually fill an entire castle.

A typical Kunstkammer (if such a thing ever existed), contained a marvellous array of objects. First, *naturalia*: amber, pearls, coral, shells, eggs, stones, and stuffed animals. Then, *mirabilia*: absurdities of nature such as malformed animal foetuses or stag heads with fantastically shaped antlers, and also materials which were believed to have therapeutic powers, to be astrologically significant, or that were regarded as aphrodisiacs, such as mandrake roots, obsidian stones, and the twisted horn of the narwhal. Also, *scientifica*: objects made from precious metals, automata, and surgical instruments, perhaps. Finally, *artificialia*: products of the human hand, including apothecaries' instruments, board games, clocks, trompe l'oeil, even toiletries and textiles. Into this category comes Laue's Dresden cherry stone with 185 faces carved on it.

Laue entered this esoteric world at the age of ten, when he began attending auctions with his father, an antiques dealer. He learnt that to succeed in the business you had to work hard and amass as much knowledge as possible, that you needed to know all about restoration, and that you had to be able to spot a fake at

RIGHT On an extravagantly carved 17th-century cabinet, Laue displays *memento mori*, which form a strong part of his collection. The globes are hand warmers, with an oil flame in the middle, used by travellers. In the top centre is a collection of 18th-century wax seals, presented as a book.

a hundred yards. He became preoccupied with Renaissance *Kunstkammern* and *Wunderkammern*, and at university he studied the subject in depth. Then he found the ideal setting for his business: a fabulous 1873 building with grand columns and a stuccoed ceiling decorated with frescoes, designed by Blersch, the Royal Bavarian court's stucco master. Laue was given carte blanche to restore the gallery to its former glory, and he turned it into an inimitable setting for his collection of unusual and impressive objects.

The perennial problem of the collector/ dealer is having to part with his precious finds, and for Laue it is no different, though he is logical and businesslike enough to cope. "Sometimes it is very hard for me to have to sell something," he says, "but

often I have pieces for quite some time, and when I sell them it gives me the opportunity to buy something else." He also relishes the opportunity to learn more about this endless subject, enjoying the chance to travel and to swap ideas with like-minded experts. Indeed, learning is what it is all about. Laue describes the central idea of all *Kunstkammer* collections as comprehending the interplay of art and nature. He adds: "Part of learning about the realm of *Kunstkammer* is learning to see, getting involved with the objects, and the world-view of a vanished era. I think the ability to empathize with other situations and eras, to view things from a different perspective in order to develop a certain aesthetic sensitivity, is an important human quality."

ABOVE Laue's gallery, with its parquet floor and stuccoed ceilings is laid out as a series of intimate and very individual rooms. In the left-hand cabinet of this room is a narwhal tusk and skull, highly prized during the Renaissance because it was believed to belong to a unicorn.

LEFT A huge collector's cabinet, probably from a pharmacy and dating to around 1700, takes pride of place in the centre of the *Kunstkammer*.

"It's an evil passion. Collectors are exactly like dope addicts: we need the next fix."

Lee B Anderson, New York, NY, USA
AMERICAN GOTHIC

The place: Paris. The date: just after World War II. Lee Anderson, a young American soldier who had been posted to England, had just arrived in the City of Light, where he met up with the eccentric writer Gertrude Stein. They decided to visit Matisse and Picasso, taking them each a gift, and to ask for a painting. Breathtaking cheek, but it worked. And so began Anderson's art collection.

He returned to the United States and became a schoolteacher; on a schoolteacher's salary he began to buy American paintings of the 18th and 19th centuries. He had a great eye, even better judgement, and an amount of daring, buying works just before they became fashionable. He did his research thoroughly, and dealt only with the best dealers, paying by instalments when necessary. And then, in 1955, he sold a small group of pictures for $2.25 million. "I invested it and became a playboy, which was all I was ever cut out to be," he jokes.

Anderson had by this time bought the 18th-century New York brownstone in which he still lives. Like his other purchases, it was a superb investment: at $10,200 it cost a great deal of money 50 years ago, but today – as he proudly tells you – it's worth $3 million. He renovated the seven-storey property himself and then he started to collect furniture with which to fill it. First classic, and then, driven away by high prices, American Gothic Revival furniture, to be precise. "Gothic is an important alternative form to classicism. I started collecting the Gothic furniture in the same way I collected paintings: it was less expensive because it was less popular," he explains. "I was buying Tiffany glass before anyone else was interested. I was always a little bit ahead of things." These days, however, plenty of people are interested in what Anderson has collected – fashion has caught up with his taste and, especially as his is probably the finest and most comprehensive such collection in the world, it is worth a great deal of money. Not only that, but museums are queuing up for bequests. Already much of Anderson's collection is on rotating loan to the Metropolitan Museum in New York, and it composed the heart of the seminal Houston Museum exhibition *The Gothic Taste in America* of 1976. "The very best is in my house," he asserts. "It's all signed and documented. This is home to me; I couldn't live any place else."

RIGHT Anderson has hundreds of Gothic Revival chairs in his New York brownstone home. His superb collection also includes a mass of other pieces, from miniatures to busts, from 18th- and 19th-century American paintings to fine tea sets.

To describe Anderson's home as full would definitely be an understatement. He has 13 rooms and, when asked how many pieces are in his collection, he reckons – only half-joking – that he has 5,000 in each room. Not only that, but the walls are covered, frame to frame, with paintings. "When you try to dust it's something else. I've got a great deal of money but I can't get a cleaning person. They just disorganize everything, so I have to do it myself."

The best pieces (though it's hard to separate out the best, as everything is superb) include an early 18th-century sketch of George Washington taken from life (he exchanged his Picasso for this), two chairs by French cabinet-maker Bouvier, and about 350 pieces of Sèvres porcelain. The collection also includes English mirrors, French inkwells, New York lamps, glass perfume bottles, sconces, busts, statuettes, vases, miniatures, tea sets, Parian ware, clocks, candelabra, curtains, rugs, and cabinets. There is an Italian room, whose walls are lined with paintings featuring views of Italy by well-known artists, and the vestiges of – wait for it – a Wild West room, which itself only lasted a couple of years, but has left a legacy of Native American artefacts and early paintings of the American West. But it is the Gothic Revival furniture for which Anderson is renowned. So much so that he has been dubbed The Godfather of Gothic. He adores the style, though he prefers to mix it with classicism and, more recently, Egyptian Revival, with which, he says, Gothic looks awfully good. He has hundreds of Gothic chairs alone, lined around rooms and along hallways, their

pointed and trefoiled shapes creating a rhythmic harmony that counterpoints the crowded, atmospheric rooms.

Not surprisingly, Anderson loves the look and feel of the great English country houses, with their accumulation of wonderful furniture from generation after generation. And although his is undeniably an American townhouse, he has achieved something of the country-house style: a unique blend of the New World and the Old, where stylistic differences matter less than the unifying eye of the man who has carefully assembled and arranged this outstanding collection.

Life without collecting would, to Anderson, be unthinkable. He has had a fantastic 50 years of it, he says. "I started when I was seven years old, and I

have collected like mad ever since. I was lucky to have a good eye, and I always did a lot of looking. I went abroad, to London and Paris, two or three times a year, and always came back loaded with new things. "Travel is the most wonderful thing. I've been around the world a couple of times, and it's been wonderful." And do you think that he has started to slow down? Not one bit of it. He may not be able to travel like he used to, but he can't stop the eternal chase, the hunt for the next great find which is just around the corner. "My collection is my life. It's an evil passion," he says. "Collectors are exactly like dope addicts: we need the next fix. I've just had my 85th birthday and I still get really excited when I buy something. Oh no, I'm not about to give up collecting."

ABOVE In the spare bedroom the magnificent bed by Alexander Roux is topped with a crewelwork throw and surrounded, naturally, by fine paintings of the 18th and 19th centuries.

natural history

OUR FASCINATION WITH NATURAL PHENOMENA HAS LED TO SOME OF THE MOST INTRIGUING COLLECTIONS OF ANCIENT AND MODERN TIMES. HERE, WE LOOK AT A SELECTION OF CONTEMPORARY COLLECTIONS, FROM TAXIDERMY TO POODLE KITSCH, BUTTERFLIES TO LIVE BIRDS, WHICH DEMONSTRATE OUR CONTINUING PASSION FOR THE ENDLESS VARIETY OF THE WORLD AROUND US.

"It's not an expensive hobby, but it's a massive investment of time."

Lawrence Forcella, Hastings-on-Hudson, NY, USA
INSECTS

There's something strange about our almost universal dislike of insects. Whether it's to do with their shiny eyes, quivering legs, or furry appendages, or perhaps the way they crawl, fly, or jump, we seem to be repulsed by them almost as intensely as we fear them.

Fortunately – just to even up the balance a little – there are a few individuals who love insects just as fiercely as the rest of us loathe them; people who admire their unusual shapes, their vivid colours, and their varied patterns; people who are intrigued by their behaviour, their diversity, and their provenance. One such is Lawrence Forcella, a young New Yorker who concentrates his professional and personal life around an intense fascination with insects, from dung beetles to tarantulas, leaf hoppers to fruit flies. Even the lowly cockroach, the bane of the Big Apple, doesn't escape his attention.

For Forcella, the collecting habit started young. He reckons he was about three years old when he found a stag beetle while playing at a friend's house in the Bronx. Encouraged by his parents, he put it in a box and kept it. As he grew older, more beetles followed (it was the sign of an inexperienced collector, however, that all too often the different elements in his collection would eat each other), but in his teens he digressed to seashells and then, at art school, he moved onto animal skulls. He amassed a collection of about 50, going so far as to find roadkills, cut off their heads, and clean them before adding them to his display. However, the lure of insects could not, eventually, be denied, and when Forcella began drawing them for his studies he started to collect them again, this time more seriously. He started to collect any form of domestic insect he could, and to buy tropical insects, too. A job at Evolution, a natural history shop in Manhattan, followed, and it wasn't long before Forcella was a fully fledged entomologist, head of a self-created department at work, with a collection bursting out of his apartment in Hastings-on-Hudson of somewhere between 5,000 and 10,000 insects. Some are alive – he likes to raise caterpillars and hatch butterflies, and to keep a few cockroaches, centipedes, and tarantulas – but mostly they're dead. Artfully arranged and then stuck on a pin, they are labelled and displayed in a way that combines the scientific and the aesthetic. "After looking at dead bugs for

RIGHT Small insects are difficult to display attractively, but anything over 5mm (¼in) can have its legs and antennae arranged before being placed in one of the many specially made wooden drawers that are stacked up in Forcella's living room.

decade after decade you do start to think about how you can make them look better," he says. But the science is important, too. Forcella won't buy anything from abroad that he can collect and label himself at home, because he believes that a collection such as his must be capable of yielding useful data to interested observers in 20, 30 or 100 years' time.

In a four-room apartment, severe limitations on space have meant that Forcella has slowed down his collecting to just the essentials, though his plan is to find a permanent display site where his pride and joy will be on view to many more people. For the meantime, however, he loves to show friends different parts of his collection, perhaps just a few drawers at a time – anything more is just overwhelming. Not surprisingly, they are fascinated, whether by the beautiful colours and shapes, or by the lives of the insects themselves, or by the sheer size of the collection and Forcella's dedication to it. "I've been doing this nearly my whole life and I've logged literally thousands of hours going out with a net, writing data tags, and arranging the insects," he explains. "It's not an expensive hobby, but it is a massive investment of time." When Forcella tells you that, what with building up the business, planning a permanent display and researching, logging, monitoring, and increasing his collection, he has no spare time, you tend to believe him. But behind his resignation is the satisfaction of a true collector, a man for whom work and life have become inextricably linked and who, if he found himself with time on his hands, would spend more of it on insects, insects, and yet more insects.

ABOVE LEFT Forcella is obsessive about logging data, and carefully labels even the tiniest of insects so that it will yield useful information to anyone who wishes to study it. However, while small bugs may hold great scientific value, the eye-catching colours and patterns show up much better on larger insects such as these lanternflies.

ABOVE Forcella has a few thousand different types of shell, which he both collects himself and buys from dealers. These examples are relatively small; his biggest is a Triton's trumpet shell that is more than a foot long.

RIGHT Rainbow-like colours are one reason beetles are among the most frequently collected insects. These are different kinds of flower beetle from around the world. Some, like the African goliath beetles at the top, reach gigantic proportions, with wingspans of 20cm (8in).

"If you dismiss the dross, how do you decide what is good?"

Alec Cobbe, East Clandon, Surrey, England
CURIOSITIES

Sometimes you just cannot escape genetics. If collecting is in your blood, there is simply no getting away from it. And collecting most certainly is in Alec Cobbe's blood. He comes from a long line of collectors – at least four or five generations – and so it could be said that it was predestination, rather than choice, that led him on this path.

Cobbe himself, a painter, designer, restorer, and architectural consultant, has two magnificent collections. One is of Old Master paintings, which began with an inheritance and to which he has added over the years. The second is of antique keyboard instruments that are linked in some way with well-known composers. He has 43 instruments, including harpsichords, pianofortes, organs, and virginals, of which a dozen were actually owned or played by great composers such as Purcell, JS Bach, Mozart, Beethoven, Liszt, Mahler, and Elgar. It is the largest such collection to be seen in one place anywhere in the world, and is displayed (along with the Old Masters) in the splendid Adam rooms at his home, Hatchlands, in Surrey, England, which is leased from the National Trust. Cobbe started this unusual collection 30 years ago, after buying a cheap old piano because he couldn't afford a new one. It turned out that it had been made by the maker of Haydn's piano, and thus he began a quest to acquire similar finds.

Paying members of the public can view these two collections during National Trust opening hours, and can even hear the instruments at one of the frequent concerts at Hatchlands, but what few of them are aware of is a third, historic, collection which is housed in Cobbe's personal sitting room. This is part of a collection of curiosities, a private museum that was put together by his 18th- and 19th-century ancestors and which Cobbe has kept together, putting some on show in its original setting at the family seat of Newbridge, outside Dublin, and transferring the rest to Surrey. Much of it is still in its 200-year-old cases. "It's the only cabinet of curiosities in the British Isles to survive with its original installation," he explains proudly.

The collection was started by one Thomas Cobbe, from 1742–65, the only surviving son of the Archbishop of Dublin. On his marriage, Thomas and his wife, Lady Betty Beresford, were given the house at Newbridge, the land around

RIGHT Cases of stuffed animals and reptiles are displayed side by side with exotic pieces such as this Indian hookah in Alec Cobbe's family collection, which was amassed over several generations during the 18th and 19th centuries.

it, and a handsome sum of money by the archbishop. They began to collect, mainly pictures, and to decorate their house with plasterwork. Three grandsons, Charles, Thomas Alexander, and the Reverend Henry William, continued the tradition, Charles from the family seat and Thomas from India. Further pieces were found in Egypt, America, the Near and Far East, and China, among them such wonders as an 18th-century Tahitian head rest, an Indian dancing whip, a wax version of Raphael's *Resurrection*, a Chinese compass, a hummingbird's nest, a Burmese prayer book on gilded papyrus, a chunk of lava from Mount Vesuvius stamped 1833, the tail of a yak, and a pair of Indian slippers decorated with beetle's wings. There is also an extensive range of shells, stuffed animals, coins, and fossils.

The collection remained intact until 1961, when the cabinets were banished to the attics and basement at Newbridge. Cobbe says: "Snakeskin hangings mingled with out-of-date carpet sweepers, and the sight of mould taking hold below stairs so

upset me, aged 15, that I rescued everything in the basement and put it in the Far Nursery for safekeeping." He had been familiar with the collection since he was a young child, always being very fond of it, and rescuing it from certain neglect seemed like the only course open to him. What Cobbe has not done, however, is to restore the collection. Much of it is incredibly fragile, but nevertheless it survives perfectly well, mostly labelled with hand-written tags. Nor has he been overly selective in how it is displayed: he describes much of the collection as junk, but enjoys the juxtaposition of the worthless with the valuable, the exotic with the familiar. This is in contrast to the modern curatorial habit of showing only a few carefully selected objects. As he says: "It's as if we printed books for adults in the very large type used for children. It's a recession of the mind. If you dismiss the dross, how do you decide what is good?" For a curious collector, especially one with collecting in his blood, even dross can have a fascination all of its own.

ABOVE Cobbe says that much of the collection is junk; nevertheless, it is fascinating junk, and includes curiosities and exotica from all over the world.

RIGHT Cobbe does not believe in showing only a few carefully selected objects, but instead enjoys the amalgamation of his ancestors' finds.

"It is a passion rather than a collection, and is related to my love of nature."

Michelle Joubert, Gignac, France
BUTTERFLIES AND BIRDS

In the history of butterfly collecting there have been many extraordinary characters. Take Colonel Frederick Markham Bailey, for example, an eccentric British spy and key protagonist in what was known as the Great Game, the late-19th-century battle of wits between the expansionist British in India and the expansionist Russians in central Asia. Markham, a kind of end-of-Empire action man, routinely disguised himself as an Austrian, Serbian, or a Romanian, despite often having little knowledge of the relevant language, and took great pleasure in the fact that his clandestine activities allowed him the chance to pursue his hobby of butterfly collecting in out of the way places.

And what about Henri Charrière, criminal and author of *Papillon* and *Banco*, a pair of semi-autobiographical novels describing his experiences in a French penitentiary? The jail's then governor was Eugene LeMoult, one of the 20th century's most important private butterfly collectors, and when Charrière was released he was encouraged to collect butterflies commercially. Charrière, however, could not resist deviating from the straight and narrow, and managed to defraud an American collector by faking a *morpho melaneus*, a specimen in which one pair of wings is female and the other male.

Then there was Margaret Fountaine, an adventurous Englishwoman who, initially nursing a broken heart, broke away from a traditional Victorian upbringing to travel the world from Turkey to Tibet, Beirut to Budapest, studying, breeding, and collecting butterflies (and also collecting lovers, but this is another story), and recording them in wonderful painted studies that are now held in the entomological library at the Natural History Museum in London.

Perhaps it is collecting per se that attracts such wonderful and intriguing characters. After all, the person in whom such passion is aroused (by the thrill of the hunt, the search for the perfect find, the joy of acquiring a long sought-after object... until the next one is required) must be a particularly interesting individual. And, indeed, at Michelle Joubert's home in the Luberon area of France there is plenty of evidence of a lively and unusual mind at work. Joubert is one of France's foremost interior decorators, and her home is an impressive 18th-century chateau which is a registered historic monument. She has restored it with

RIGHT In the library, beautifully made cases of butterflies line ranks of shelves. The owls perched on top are Joubert's favourite part of her collection.

ABOVE Joubert's aim is to keep the memory of the animals alive, and so she loves to show off a menagerie of small creatures in glass-fronted book cabinets.

RIGHT Joubert particularly loves her tiny birds. Meanwhile, the gorgeous colours and repetitive shapes of the elegantly displayed butterflies appeal to her decorator's eye.

great attention to historical authenticity, with beautiful fireplaces, tiled floors, and charming antique furnishings. But it is not the chateau itself, nor its furnishings, that are so remarkable. It is that Joubert's private rooms (some rooms are rented to guests on luxury food and wine holidays) are filled with an assortment of stuffed birds and small animals, and an array of butterflies in cases, all displayed in the most elegant way imaginable. Carefully framed cases of butterflies line specially made shelves in her library, in front of which stand tiny birds. In other rooms, glass-fronted bookcases also house a mini-menagerie, or else a succession of birds and mammals parade over bureaux or across the floor.

Joubert is entranced by her collection, which numbers 100 birds, 180 boxes of butterflies, six elephants, and numerous small creatures, and is growing all the time. She started collecting ten years ago, with some butterflies she came across in an antiques shop, and found that she could not stop. She hunts everywhere to acquire new finds, adding: "It is a passion rather than a collection, and is related to my love of nature." Some of her butterfly species are now extinct, so although the collection has the appearance of an elegantly thought-out still life, a sort of accessory to Joubert's gorgeous castle, it also has a sound lepidopterical purpose. Margaret Fountaine would have been impressed.

ABOVE Are they real or stuffed? Joubert's collection is, at times, so life-like it is hard to tell. The birds and animals are a quirky accessory to the historically authentic furnishings of the 18th-century chateau's interior.

"You have to be creative with the display or it would just look like a mound of junk."

Chuck Hettinger & Frank Carabineris, New York, NY, USA
POODLE KITSCH

Try as hard as you might, you would be hard put to find any collectors who get as much fun from their passion as New Yorkers Chuck Hettinger and Frank Carabineris. Veering madly from kitsch to high art and back again, their collection is a demonstration of their love for one particular canine breed: the poodle. Hettinger and Carabineris own two real-life standard poodles themselves (no toy variety, these are BIG dogs – head turners, in fact, especially when wearing their studded leather harnesses). "Niagara arrived in 1995 and August two years later, and somewhere in between we got our first poodle cookie jar," says Hettinger. "That's what started the whole thing off."

They were, in any case, keen collectors. When they moved in together they had to amalgamate Hettinger's collection of Judy Jetson memorabilia with Carabineris' Victoriana. They also collect cookie jars in general, 20th-century furniture, ceramics, Niagara Falls memorabilia, Blenko glassware – the really big bottles – and religious artefacts. "But our poodle collection is the silliest."

They go to the flea market more or less every week – though these days they already have so much stuff it has to be something pretty special for them to go for it – and when they travel they always seek out antiques fairs and shops. What has surprised them, though, is the ease with which they have found poodle pieces. "There's a zillion poodle things," says Hettinger. "The range is amazing, it really runs the gamut from the sublime to the ridiculous. A lot of poodle pieces are functional, because of the shape. We have a perfume bottle cover, for example, and a pair of 1960s poodle-headed boot trees, which are fantastic. I use them for my Dolce & Gabbana biker boots and I just love that juxtaposition." They also have children's books, postcards, drawings, paintings and prints, towels, stuffed toys, plaster figurines, soap dishes, and even a poodle-shaped magazine rack, among other things. On the whole, the collection dates from the second half of the 20th century, and is composed of relatively everyday items, though they do have a pencil drawing that dates to 1899, a bronze by renowned early 20th-century animal sculptor Madeleine Park, and a couple of quite valuable limited edition Peteena the Poodle dolls by Hasbro from 1966. It is, in general, light-hearted in style. "The poodle is the smartest, most sophisticated

RIGHT A panoply of poodles, from pencil drawings to stuffed toys, figurines to towels, adds canine cheer to the downstairs bathroom in Hettinger and Carabineris' New York apartment.

and most loyal companion you could have, very noble but extremely maligned in most eyes and portrayed as a clown," says Hettinger. "What I like about our collection is seeing the different ways that people perceive the poodle. It really represents the widest range of the collecting world."

As with most collectors, Hettinger, a decorative painter, and Carabineris, an office manager ("I'm visual, he's practical," says the former), have had to work almost as hard on displaying their collection as on putting it together. In some ways harder, because their poodle pieces often seemed to find them rather than the other way around. As Hettinger explains: "Oh, you have to be creative with the display, or it would just look like a mound of junk." Their big decision was to group all their poodle

pieces together in their downstairs bathroom, which meant clearing out the religious artefacts. "We painted the room white and replaced the Virgin Mary with an Italian ceramic poodle." The pieces, gathered over the succeeding years, have been grouped on the floors, walls, and shelves, a poodle panorama that adds a note of cheer to an otherwise plain room. Every now and then, they give generously to a local charity shop; they also rent elements of their collection to prop stylists for film and photographic shoots. Their pair's biggest headache, however, is how to stop their friends from contributing to the ever-growing collection. "We've tried to tell them that we don't really collect poodle pieces," laughs Hettinger. "But for some reason they don't seem to believe us."

ABOVE Everything in the bathroom, right down to the soap and the toothbrush holders, is decorated with poodles. On the whole, the collection is composed of everyday, light-hearted pieces from the second half of the 20th century.

LEFT Niagara, one of the guys' two standard poodles, poses alongside the collection. Before the poodles took over, the bathroom was full of religious artefacts.

"It became so crowded with our collections that we had to walk sideways down the corridor."

Tim Knox & Todd Longstaffe-Gowan, London, England
HISTORICAL COLLECTIONS

To place Tim Knox and Todd Longstaffe-Gowan in any single category of collecting is perhaps to miss the point of the extraordinary collections that they have brought together in more than a decade spent in the passionate pursuit of all manner of objects. While it is true that they have assembled a remarkable group of natural history specimens, architectural fragments and models, pictures and sculpture, and other curiosities, their aim has been far richer and more complex than that of simply amassing rooms full of quirky objects. As much scholars as collectors, they share a serious interest in the history of collecting, and they have sought to form a collection that evokes the feel of the great private museums of the past, arranging their treasures in a deliberately theatrical manner.

By coincidence both grew up in exotic places, and both from an early age became inveterate collectors. They were at first drawn in particular to shells and other natural curiosities, but rapidly diversified into other areas rich in numinous objects, including religious statuary and relics. Several years spent as a curator in the celebrated drawings collection of the Royal Institute of British Architects honed Knox's interest in and deep knowledge of English architecture; now, as the National Trust's head curator, he is much concerned with the investigation of historic interiors and collections and their preservation. Todd Longstaffe-Gowan is a garden designer and historian. His love of sculpture and his fascination for the natural world are combined with a grand sense of scale, which he brings to all their arrangements.

As their collection continued to grow in various locations, filling the available space ever more densely, the collectors came to realize that a setting of suitable size and character was required to do it justice. "We were living in a mansion block in north London, which became so crowded that places to sit were at a premium, and we had to walk sideways down the corridor to reach the bathroom." Something had to give. The great break came when they found a derelict but nevertheless superb mid-18th-century merchant's townhouse in the East End of London. It had not been lived in since World War I and, having sunk to light industrial use – as a metal-foil printers and typewriter repair workshop, with the Stepney Chamber of Commerce meeting upstairs – it had been

RIGHT In one of the main museum-like rooms, stuffed birds, big game trophies, skeletons, and architectural models jostle for space. On a plinth in the foreground stands the skull of an elephant, better than any Henry Moore sculpture.

LEFT In the entrance hall, the walls have been stripped down to the old, discoloured paint, which provides an atmospheric backdrop for a plaster bust, portrait roundels, and stags' heads.

ABOVE A collection of portrait busts in the Sarcophagus Room. The colossal marble bust in the centre is of Maurice of Nassau, Prince of Orange, and a pair to one in the Palace of Het Loo in Holland.

RIGHT The original panelling and paint in the drawing room were preserved under layers of hessian and wallpaper. The centre portrait, of a man with a hare lip, is by Adriaen Carpentière, c.1762. The stuffed goat is probably Indian, though, mysteriously, it wears a dog collar inscribed Kelveden.

ABOVE A collection of
stuffed dogs in a bedroom,
combined with saccharine
19th-century oleographs of
religious subjects.

condemned for demolition. It was filthy and squalid beyond belief, and desperately needed loving owners who were prepared to restore it to its former glory – which is exactly what Knox and Longstaffe-Gowan proceeded to do.

The restoration of the house and the installation of the collection have gone on simultaneously over the last five years. For some considerable time workmen, building materials, and statuary came and went from the house almost simultaneously. The first task was to remove the shops which had been built out at the front of the house, where they had filled in the basement and the front garden and obscured the lower floors. Fragments of surviving panelling were copied and recreated, chimneypieces installed and, in some cases, the ceilings, floors, and walls rebuilt. The

aim was to bring back the spirit and life of the house, working with it rather than against it, preserving where possible and faithfully recreating where not.

Just as importantly, the owners wanted to create a magnificent setting for their collection, one which complemented its eclectic and unusual feel and which would provide a backdrop that was neither too eye-catching nor too bland. That this has, unquestionably, worked, is proved by the fact that one hardly knows where their furniture ends and the collection begins. Into the house they brought their wonders, from portraits of princes to papal indulgences, some priceless, some worth just pennies. To give more than a flavour of this extensive and unusual collection is virtually impossible. It ranges from the ancient world to the contemporary,

from Egypt to Cornwall, and from natural specimens to man-made wonders. In one of the large reception rooms Knox and Longstaffe-Gowan's stuffed bird collection is installed, stacked up one glass case atop another in the traditional style of the British country house. It is complemented by a Gothic sideboard from a John Nash castle in Ireland, a recently acquired ostrich skeleton, and various trophy heads, including one of a bull giraffe. In the bathroom are hung crucifixes and embossed Victorian memorial pictures. In another room, called the museum, are death masks, life masks of Knox and Longstaffe-Gowan, and a portion of the vertebra of King James II of England. More marvels are to be seen at every turn, all arranged with exquisite care and taste. It is hardly a surprise that Knox and Longstaffe-Gowan

describe themselves as fanatic collectors and researchers, or to learn that this is a project that still has great potential to expand and change. The house needs more work, and meanwhile the collection will never stand still – the collectors live and breathe the hunt for interesting trophies, and spend every available moment looking for new discoveries. So far, they have found Bertel Thorvaldsen's lost marble bust of Sir Walter Scott, Gainsborough's earliest full-length portrait, two drawings by Christopher Wren, and a highly important 17th-century drawing of the font at Canterbury Cathedral – found lying in the rain on a barrow in London's Portobello Road. But then, this pair are specialists in finding beauty, value, and significance in places that ordinary mortals would simply pass by.

ABOVE **The Bird Room** was once a typewriter repair workshop. Knox and Longstaffe-Gowan's stuffed bird collection is displayed here, with boxes stacked à la country house. The giraffe was discovered years ago in a skip and, somewhat battered and missing an ear, was later given to Longstaffe-Gowan.

NEXT PAGE Another view of the Drawing Room. Two painted wooden statues of Our Lady of the Sorrows flank an overmantel filled with reliquaries.

"I am attracted to the sheer beauty of things and I enjoy having them around me."

Mary Jo McConnell, Old Marblehead, MA, USA
ANTHROPOLOGICAL FINDS

In the mountain regions of Papua New Guinea lives a small bird known as the Vogelkop, or bowerbird. The species is unique in that it spends its time building – with enormous care – a conspicuous bower, adorned with natural substances such as berries, moss, flowers, and dead beetles, as well as scavenged man-made items such as tin cans. In fact, the local tribal word for bowerbird translates as "he who collects things and puts them in piles". Ornithologists believe that the purpose of these bowers is to attract a female; for Boston-based artist Mary Jo McConnell, however, there is a more intriguing explanation. Every year, McConnell travels to a remote region of the Arfak mountains of Irian Jaya, western New Guinea, to document the activities of a group of bowerbirds, in a quest to demonstrate that the birds are functioning just like artists, each with a particular style and colour palette. She has named some of the birds she observes – Van Gogh, Warhol, Klee, Matisse, Leonardo – and traces the progress of their constructions from year to year, whether it be the addition of a blue can, placed next to a yellow can with blue detailing, or the arrangement of glittering, amber-like, sap crystals in a pile next to some shiny black beetles.

In a place off-limits to most outsiders, McConnell is welcomed by the villagers, who recognize her as an admirer, rather than a destroyer, of nature. She spends hours sitting alone in the forest, watching, marvelling at, and treasuring the unspoilt world around her, and painting the birds at work, collecting information about what she sees as their aesthetic decisions. Though her process is in some ways scientific, it is always governed by her artistic instincts, which she identifies as being very much in line with those of the bowerbirds – chiefly, the desire to collect attractive things and to embellish her environment with them. Beauty always comes first, she says.

Back home in Old Marblehead, north of Boston, McConnell shares her rambling, 17th-century house on the harbour with a variety of collections, including beetles, feathers, eggs and stuffed birds, paintings, and ethnic sculptures. It is a private gallery filled with anthropological and archaeological treasures: woodcarvings from Haiti, Balinese combs and wooden figures, tribal masks and headdresses from New Guinea. These treasures were amassed from years of

RIGHT McConnell's collections are arranged instinctively; here they cram the walls and staircase of her 17th-century home north of Boston. She has Indonesian combs, sculptures from New Guinea, paintbrushes, and her own monoprints of feathers.

ABOVE "Everything just goes where it should go," says McConnell. In the glass treasure chest is a selection of hats from Africa, Indonesia, and Borneo, while in front of it is a giant carved wooden fish from Indonesia.

RIGHT The prints of feathers and eggs are McConnell's own work. She also has real eggs, nests, and stuffed birds – which some visitors are hard put to differentiate from the 15 live birds that perch around the house among her collections.

adventurous travelling around the world, though, as McConnell points out, without her ever having made a conscious decision to collect – "I'm attracted to the sheer beauty of things and I enjoy having them around me." Among these inanimate objects can be found McConnell's 15 or so live birds, exotic creatures that include an African hornbill called Milly (whom McConnell has owned for 20 years), a hummingbird from Peru, an Amazonian parrot from Haiti, toucans from South America, and Bolivian macaws. This particular collection exists because McConnell is concerned for the survival of their species: "Birds must be established in captivity for future avicultur-ists and the protection of the species themselves in case of increased loss of habitat," she says.

Of course, as well as the environmental benefits, McConnell simply adores her birds, who are her friends and who also provide her with constant artistic stimulation. Rather than simply painting their portraits, however, her work is inspired by colour and form, and employs various media. McConnell's art reflects her love for and fascination with objects of wonder, a private world which she has created around her and which she recreates in her paintings. A private world which is, if you like, parallel to that of the bowerbirds with whom she identifies so strongly. "The bowerbirds are interested in the same things that I am," she says. "Colour, collecting, and arranging. When you see a bowerbird at work he knows exactly where things should go."

ABOVE McConnell has built birdcages all around her home, but on the whole her birds prefer to perch and fly outside. She believes that keeping birds in the home is hugely educational. "We all live in some sort of cage, but to share the same space, food, and day with birds in an intimate setting is a great honour, very grounding, and a good place to sort out cultural and natural boundaries."

eccentricities and curiosities

UNUSUAL, WITTY, OUTRAGEOUS, SURPRISING, EYE-CATCHING, INTRIGUING, AND EVEN DOWNRIGHT BIZARRE, SOME COLLECTIONS SIMPLY CANNOT BE FITTED INTO ANY CONVENTIONAL CATEGORY. YET THEY ARE JUST AS IMPRESSIVE, ATTRACTIVE, AND WONDERFUL – WHETHER FEATURING JAPANESE PLASTIC TOYS, ROYAL MEMORABILIA, OR OLD AEROPLANE PARTS – AS ANY OF THE MORE CONSERVATIVE GENRES OF COLLECTING.

"I wanted to create a living museum, where the public live and dream as much as they simply visit."

Jean-Paul Favand, Paris, France
FESTIVAL ART

It comes as no surprise to learn that Jean-Paul Favand's collection is a favourite of television shows – it is visually stunning, a colourful, evocative feast that grabs in an immediate, emotional way and does not want to let go. His is a collection that unites art, life, and dreams, a collection of objects to do with festivals, carnivals, spectacles, and performance – the largest in Europe. It is a private museum that is occasionally open to the public, or can be booked for groups of visitors, conferences, or private parties, the latter with performances by acrobats, musicians, puppeteers, and actors that bring their surroundings to life.

The museum is based at Les Pavillons de Bercy, a 19th-century former wine merchant's depot in eastern Paris, where it is spread over a vast space of 1,800 sq m (19,300 sq ft). Its scale and diversity is awe-inspiring. There are three main themes. The first, mechanical music, occupies several rooms decorated in a grand style, and is a surreal fusion of music hall, opera house, and theatre from the early 20th century. Here can be seen pianos, nickelodeons, and music boxes, a 1934 pipe organ, an electronic dance organ, and a fairground organ, all watched over by the wax figures of famous turn-of-the-century opera- and concert-goers, from Debussy to Toulouse-Lautrec, Victor Hugo to Sarah Bernhardt. Here, too, one can play games of chance, have one's fortune told, or try a test of strength, with a collection of games and stalls that demonstrate popular life at the beginning of the Belle Epoque.

The second theme is that of fairground art, a collection which is one of the most important in the world. Favand has gathered 14 carousels, 16 stalls (shooting galleries, wheels of fortune, games of chance, and so on), 18 ensembles (historical sub-collections on a common theme), and more than 1,500 individual items, including sculpture, marionettes, distorting mirrors, and gaming tables. The objects date from 1850–1950, the heyday of the fairground, which united the mechanical developments of the Industrial Revolution with medieval art forms and traditions. These rooms which, despite their size, can only show about one-fifth of the collection, are a splendidly colourful fusion of the different styles that inspired fairground artists, including Rococo, Baroque, Art Nouveau, and Art Deco.

ABOVE The music rooms are decorated in a style which fuses that of music halls, opera houses, and theatres. The largest room contains an automatic piano played by a model of Victor Hugo.

RIGHT Fairground art encompassed all the popular art forms of the day in a spectacular and gaudy style that knew no limits.

NEXT The Pavillons de Bercy cannot show Favand's entire collection. In storage, the carved animals from fairground rides are stacked dramatically, pawing the ground as if alive.

The third theme is of Venetian carnival and street theatre. Favand has reconstructed a magnificent 18th-century Venetian palazzo, complete with masked model figures in authentic costumes standing on balconies, surrounded by gilded torchères. Antique scenery is used for performances in which costumed figures act out a masquerade as gondolas sail past. Outside is a piazza in which a troupe of touring acrobats has set up for a performance.

It has taken Favand more than 20 years of detailed research and painstaking restoration to put this extraordinary collection together. He travelled all over Europe, studied thousands of historical documents, and consulted any number of experts, from musicians to fairground owners. The restoration work, sometimes involving months on one single piece, required 20 craftsmen specializing in fields as varied as art restoration, painting, gilding, sculpting, mechanics, and metalwork; incredibly, all the objects in the museum are in full working order. It was always Favand's aim to present the collection to the public: after all, without an audience neither music, fairgrounds, or carnival would exist. He wants, above all, to reunite us with the idea of escaping from the daily grind to a world of wonder and enchantment. "As day-to-day life becomes more hurried and impersonal, the idea of festivals has all but disappeared," he says. "My personal dream was to bring the idea of festivals and spectacles alive in the present, and to preserve them for the future. I wanted to create a living museum, where the public live and dream as much as they simply visit."

"To me the Royal Family are part of the fabric of life. They are in our psyche."

Margaret Tyler, London, England
ROYAL MEMORABILIA

To call Margaret Tyler a royalist is a bit like calling the pope a Catholic. It's true, but it doesn't really tell the whole story. Because Tyler is a staunch royalist; a loyal and devoted royalist; acknowledged as the world's number one fan of the British Royal Family.

"Apart from my children and grandchildren, the Royal Family are the most important thing in my life," says Tyler. And she has proved it by amassing an enormous collection of royal memorabilia – more than 7,000 items – ranging from plates and mugs to paperweights and matchboxes, via books, paintings, photographs, dolls, and soft toys. It all began in Tyler's childhood. Her parents were royalists, and she developed an avid interest in the lives of the royals from around the time of the Queen's coronation in 1953 (the family didn't own a television back then, and she was broken-hearted that she couldn't watch the grand event). "You've got weddings, births, funerals – it's just like an extension of your own family," maintains Tyler. "I loved the Royal Family when I was a child, and I still do. The attraction never waned. In fact, if anything it got worse – or better, depending on which way you look at it. To me, the Royal Family are part of the fabric of life. They are in our psyche. There's a magic about them, and you can't help but be in awe of them."

She began her collection with the purchase of a small glass dish, which cost just 2½ pence, around the time of Charles and Diana's wedding in 1981. From there, it just grew and grew. Margaret used to work around the corner from Covent Garden market, so she picked things up there more or less every week, and after a while she decided to devote a room in her house to her collection. "With four small children it wasn't ideal," she admits, "but it became my little area." She acquired many of her larger pieces from a royal exhibition at Windsor that was dismantled a few years ago. Now, she often buys on a whim – like the time she bought up the entire Andrew-and-Fergie window display from a charity shop, or when she saw the owner of another shop drinking from a royal mug and just had to buy it from him. And she is also well known around the world, making TV appearances and commenting on royal occasions, so she finds that people send her pieces out of the blue.

RIGHT **The Silver Jubilee Room, devoted to souvenirs of the Queen's first 25 years on the throne. The mugs extend around all four walls of the room, while photographs, dishes, plates, stuffed corgis, and all sorts of other mementoes are arranged in every corner.**

The collection burgeoned and, with her children grown-up, Tyler has been able to devote almost her entire 1930s mock-Tudor house in North London to her passion, which is arranged chronologically and by subject. The entrance hall contains souvenirs from the weddings of Princes Andrew and Edward, while the sitting room, known as the Silver Jubilee Room, contains mementoes of the 25th anniversary of the Queen's reign in 1977. There's also a corner for the Golden Jubilee of 2002, and sections for memorabilia from Princess Anne's two weddings. The garage has been converted into the Queen Victoria Room, and holds anything relating to Victoria and succeeding generations of the early 20th century, including King George VI and Queen Elizabeth.

Tyler's two favourite royals, however, are the Queen Mother and Princess Diana. Plans are afoot to build an extension for Tyler's collection of Queen Mother memorabilia, while Diana already has a room to herself, set up as a shrine after her death in 1997. The room is covered in photographs and other mementoes of the world's most famous royal. Tyler's favourite piece is a painting of the Princess with her two sons, copied from a famous photograph, a birthday present from her children.

"People ask where I live; I live right in the middle of it," says Tyler. Even her breakfast room, where occasional royal-loving bed-and-breakfast guests enjoy a right royal fry-up, is furnished with royal caricature egg cups, crown jewels tea cosies, rows of teapots commemorating various royal events, and, most impressively of all, life-sized cut-outs of the monarch and her family. Tyler feels completely at home in such elevated company. "It looks as though the royals have come for tea," she laughs. I never feel lonely."

ABOVE LEFT Tyler's bed-and-breakfast guests enjoy their meals in good company. Tyler doesn't drive, and although large purchases are usually delivered in a van, she carried the Prince Charles cut-out home on the Underground, wrapped in a large plastic bag.

ABOVE All the crockery is royal-related, whether a serious commemorative teapot or a caricature egg cup.

RIGHT The Princess Diana Room, with the painting that Tyler's children bought for her in pride of place. The carpet is from the Lanesborough Hotel, where Diana was a regular visitor.

"People who have an artistic bent see something in the toys that gets them on a deep level."

Coop, Los Angeles, CA, USA
JAPANESE TOYS

The genre of collecting has room for many variants, and one of the wonderful things about this tradition, which goes back thousands of years, is that it is constantly evolving and changing. Thus, collecting thousands of brightly coloured, 1970s plastic toys from Japan is just as valid as collecting, say, antique busts of classical heroes. Or indeed, if the basis of collecting is to savour the unique, the curious, and the inimitable from the many corners of the globe and display the results with flair and enjoyment, then collecting Japanese toys is evidently very much a continutation of the tradition – however far from traditional it may seem.

Chris Cooper (known as "Coop") has a collection of Japanese toys that amounts to nigh on 3,000 (though he has lost track of the exact number) – a sizeable figure, even for someone who has been collecting for more than a decade. He displays them en masse (there is really no other way) in his Los Angeles home and studio, and has recently rented a 185 sq m (2,000 sq ft) loft space that will give him more room for work and – naturally – to display his collection. It's a non-stop game. The warriors, dinosaurs, undersea monsters, robots, and other fantastic creatures just seem to multiply uncontrollably, the result of Cooper's insatiable searching in local stores and on the Internet. Only a couple of weeks after these pictures were taken, for example, he took delivery of ten boxes of toys that he had ordered from one of his suppliers. "And you've got to display them properly," he says. "I know a serious collector who keeps all his pieces in his garage, but I just don't see the point of having them if you can't look at them and enjoy them." Even so, Cooper has to admit that about a third of his collection has had to be put in storage.

"It all started when I was a kid," he explains. "Mattel introduced some Japanese toys, Shogun Warriors, in America, and I was given some. When I was older I saw them again and became interested. I started off buying the pieces I'd had as a kid. When I moved to California in 1989 I was buying stuff, but I didn't get heavy-duty serious until about 1995."

Cooper lived near Little Tokyo, where he came across a store that imported Japanese toys. He was immediately fascinated, and would buy small

RIGHT The majority of Cooper's collection of *chogokin* diecast metal toys – about 300 pieces – is arranged with meticulous care in this incredible display case.

pieces now and then – for maybe eight dollars or less – "and slowly I got obsessed".

For Cooper, an artist and illustrator whose work has been described as "underground hot rod girlie monster art", his hobby feeds right into his work, in style and, sometimes, content. "Most of the people I know who collect Japanese toys are either artists or designers," he says. "I think that people who have an artistic or creative bent see something in the toys that gets to them on a deep level. I've been a record collector since I was a kid, and I buy lots of books; there are a lot of things I'm interested in. But with the toys specifically there's just some- thing about the way they look; they're beautiful objects – you can look at them and look at them, and always find something interesting."

For Cooper, the toys have a different resonance to their American or European counter- parts, a fascination due to their mythological origins. While the monsters of Europe and the USA, which spring from the ancient forest, are all fur and teeth, the monsters of Japan – very much an island culture – are aquatic in origin, perhaps based on crustacea, fish, or sea-mammals, with fins, scales, and shells.

Cooper also enjoys the fact that these precious pieces, so sought after, highly regarded, and lovingly displayed, were actually made as disposable objects, to be played with for a year or two at most, then thrown away. "When you find one that's in per- fect shape it's pretty neat," he explains. "Although in fact a lot of the vinyl toys that I have are very well used – little kids have obviously played with them,

and I really like that, too. What's more, he explains, some toys have their young owner's name handwritten on a foot – something which some collectors see as devaluing the piece, but which for him is an extra element of history and interest.

One of Cooper's favourite pieces is a character that he describes as one of the holy grails of Japanese toys. It is a diecast version of Tetsujin-28, about 40cm (16in) tall, with body panels that are magnetically attached. "Every little detail does something," he says. "It really is a work of art more than a toy." Another favourite is a perfect 135cm (54in) replica of the 20cm (8in) toy Kanegan, who has a head like an oyster shell with antennae. "Due to manufacturing problems, only five or six were ever made to this size. They were just not gettable," says

Cooper. "But then one day I went into a Japanese toy store in LA and they had one as a store display. The manager wasn't in, so the kid working there took my number and promised to ask him to ring me. All weekend I freaked out waiting for the call. I went in on the Tuesday and it turned out the manager had never been given my number."

The end of Cooper's story will be familiar to any dedicated collector – whether he or she prefers artefacts from the ancient world or the modern, animate or inanimate, animal, vegetable, or mineral. "I was determined to have it, and eventually the manager agreed to sell it to me. It was more money than I have ever paid for anything in my life, but as I handed over my credit card I was crazed with happiness."

ABOVE This is Cooper's studio, where he is surrounded by toys of all shapes, styles, and sizes. His new studio should be able to accommodate even more.

NEXT PAGE Cooper has a comprehensive collection of *sofubi* representations of various members of the Ultraman family.

"What I love about all the American stuff from this era is that everything was bigger and better."

Colin Hobden, Swanley, Kent, England
1950s AMERICANA

In a corner of otherwise unremarkable suburban southern England, there is one house that stands out from the rest. Far from being furnished with traditional three-piece suites, patterned wallpaper, and net curtains, Colin Hobden's home is an homage to 1950s America – a time and a place where the kids were cool, the music was hot, the colours were bright, and everything seemed young, fun, and optimistic.

For Hobden, it is entirely normal to live with a kitchen dedicated to Elvis Presley, a front room that's all Marilyn Monroe, a Hollywood bedroom, and stairs and landings themed à la James Dean. It has built up gradually and, as he puts it, got out of hand about four or five years ago. "I've always collected things," he explains. "You've got to have a hobby. When people decorate, they do it to their own taste. I've just done it with the things that I like. First I got myself a classic car – a 1952 Pontiac chieftain – then I got a 1950s Bal Ami jukebox, then I bought a pinball machine. I have a room at the back of the house and I kept putting things in there, but it was frustrating because there wasn't enough room to show them. Then I started to put things in the kitchen. My wife's an Elvis fan so it was natural to theme it around Elvis."

First one room, then another. Hobden collected James Dean memorabilia for the hallway and stairs (he now has 200 pictures of Dean, leaving no wall space at all), then Marilyn pieces that he assembled in the living room. Later, the bedroom turned all Hollywood glamour, the garage acquired old US petrol pumps and enamel signs and – the *pièce de résistance* – Hobden installed an old caravan in the garden which he renovated and transformed into a Marilyn Monroe-themed diner.

Like any true collector, Hobden loves the thrill of the chase, and always has an eye open for potential acquisitions, spending any spare money he has on building up his home-cum-museum. Though he says, with a tinge of regret, that he has now run out of rooms to theme. He has found a great number of his wonderful pieces through small ads in the local paper, though some have come from dealers, fairs, or other collectors. And ingenuity has played a large part in transforming his finds. The diner's shop dummy waitress, for example, was

RIGHT Hobden's kitchen is themed around the King of rock 'n' roll – Elvis Presley. In the cabinet, which was once used to display dough-nuts, are scores of small souvenirs. The fridge is a standard one which Hobden sprayed red.

NEXT PAGE The two-berth caravan, a wreck when bought, has been transformed into a fabulous American diner, and now takes up most of the small garden. The motorbike came from a fairground ride.

bought at a car boot sale, dressed in an army outfit. Hobden designed and made a new costume for her and put her on roller skates. Even more admirable, however, was the way in which he transformed a wrecked old two-berth caravan, which had been standing in a relative's neighbour's garden for more than ten years, into a delightful American diner – partly for his children and partly, naturally, for himself. Having stripped it, then painted and polished the outside, Hobden set about filling the inside with gleaming chrome chairs, a table, coffee machine, and mountains of memorabilia. The result is stunning.

"I really love the diners – the chrome, the colours, and everything," says Hobden. "What I love about all the American stuff from this era is that everything was bigger and better. They were so over the top." For a collector with a passion, what better aim than to pursue the over-the-top and then to surround oneself with it, living in an environment that is always exciting? "Well, I don't really notice it any more," says Hobden modestly. "It's just a way of life."

ABOVE Statuettes and photographs of Marilyn Monroe make up just some of the memorabilia that fills Hobden's front room.

LEFT In the diner, a waitress dummy is always on hand to serve a burger, and bottles of coke stand ready on the table. A collection of jukebox-shaped money-boxes is ranged along a high shelf behind.

RIGHT The diner is compact but has room for four chrome chairs and a table, a coffee machine, and plenty of memorabilia.

"We saw five buildings in a junk shop for a few dollars. Then we would come back with 30 or 40."

David Weingarten & Margaret Majua, Oakland, CA, USA
MODEL BUILDINGS

When David Weingarten and Margaret Majua want to see the architectural wonders of the world, they don't have to travel far. In fact, it's just a short walk from their northern California ranch house to the barn that Weingarten renovated 13 years ago, in which is housed the Empire State Building, the Eiffel Tower, the Parthenon, Gaudí's Sagrada Familia, the Great Pyramid, and Cologne Cathedral – all in miniature. Weingarten and Majua are collectors of souvenir buildings, and theirs is the best collection in private hands, numbering more than 3,000 scaled-down architectural delights.

Perhaps not surprisingly, Weingarten is an architect himself (with his partner, Lucia Howard – who also collects souvenir buildings – he heads Ace Architects in Oakland, California), while Majua runs shops that specialize in another souvenir staple: refrigerator magnets. The pair met in 1984 and began collecting in earnest in the early 1990s, though the story actually began much earlier than that, when Weingarten was still a student, travelling through Europe with his uncle, the eminent post-modern architect Charles Moore. In the German Rhine town of Speyer they toured a fine Romanesque cathedral, and found inside it a souvenir shop with two sizes of gold-coloured miniatures of the building. Moore, an inveterate collector of all kinds of ephemera, bought the larger for himself, and for Weingarten the smaller. "The little church lingered, like a virus that didn't completely infect, until a couple of years later when Margaret and I were in Monterey visiting my parents," recalls Weingarten. "We saw five buildings in a junk shop for a few dollars each that we thought would look cute with the church," says Majua. "So we brought them home. Then we started taking trips to Los Angeles, where you could once find all sorts of things, and we would come back with 30 or 40 pieces."

Today, the collection fills 100 m (300 ft) of shelves in the aforementioned barn, which Weingarten virtually rebuilt specifically for the souvenirs, each shelf finished with a thin strand of picture wire along the front to prevent the models from falling off in an earthquake. Piranesi prints line the pitched roof, and various tables and countertops provide extra space for the displays, which are lovingly designed by Weingarten, who decides where each new find should be

RIGHT Among the most sought-after (and scarcest) souvenir buildings are 1930s vintage replicas of New York's Chrysler Building. Here, a variety of these, made into paperweights, pencil sharpeners, even cigarette lighters, hover over a sea of more common miniatures of the Empire State Building.

ABOVE In 2001–2 nearly 1,000 miniatures from Ace Architects' collection were exhibited at San Francisco Airport. This vitrine contains a variety of Italian souvenirs, including the Leaning Tower of Pisa and the Campanile in Venice. There are also more obscure buildings, such as the Santa Casa in Loreto, a small sacred structure that, legend holds, angels carried from the Holy Land to Loreto in the 13th century.

RIGHT This group of Chicago souvenir buildings features, above, replicas of the Administration Building from the 1892 Colombian Exposition. This great domed monument, designed by the country's then most famous architect, Richard Morris Hunt, was pulled down at the conclusion of the fair. Its miniatures, however, including these examples produced as a clock case, coin bank, and inkwell, still survive.

placed. Majua, meanwhile, does much of the tracking down of pieces. Most of the souvenirs, generally cast in metal, clay, plastic, glass, or plaster, are between 20 and 100 years old – if not actually antiques, they are definitely serious collectibles, some worth several thousand dollars.

Weingarten speaks eloquently of the appeal of these miniatures, of the pleasure of holding a great building in one's hands and of being able to observe its details from all angles. "Souvenir buildings, in this way, provide jolts of architectural essence," he says. "Not all souvenir buildings are of great or well-known edifices, however. In Europe, souvenir buildings are landmarks. In America, a lot of souvenir buildings are places you've never heard of, like grain

silos, or a bank in Keokuk, Iowa. These lowly models were made to commemorate such events as the opening of an insurance company, and hold as much interest for Weingarten and Majua as their more illustrious counterparts. Nor do the pair differentiate between a souvenir building that is nothing but an idle ornament, and those that serve also as pencil sharpeners, lamps, thermometers, or bookends. In fact, they love the improbability of these things, the whole world distilled into one tiny model. "Think of the necessary things not yet made as souvenir buildings – toasters and coffee makers, television sets and washing machines," urges Weingarten, tongue in cheek. "Isn't it easy to see the glorious future of souvenir buildings in the next millennium?"

ABOVE German metal casters in the 1920s and 1930s were prolific makers of souvenir buildings. Among the most popular were several of the monuments symbolic of Nazism. Among other examples pictured in this group are the Volkerschlachtdenkmal in Leipzig and Kaiser Wilhelm Denkmal in Koblenz.

NEXT PAGE "A souvenir building by itself is lonely-looking," says Weingarten. The collection is housed in a small, simple, wood frame building, whose walls teem with thousands of souvenir buildings.

"I wanted to create an environment where my friends will never forget my invitations."

Frédéric Jullien, Tigeaux, France

AERONAUTICA

These days, conventional letterheads consist of a name, address, and telephone number, maybe fax and mobile contacts and, often, an email address. Not many of us follow all this with a helistation address as well. Frédéric Jullien does. And this is a clue – a rather big clue – to his lifelong passion and the nature of his collection.

Jullien is an aviator, and a pretty good one at that. He became a helicopter pilot in his mid twenties and, not long afterwards, gained a place in the French team for the World Helicopter Championships in Chantilly. Such was his enthusiasm that he soon decided to turn one room of his farm in Tigeaux, a village in central France, into a clubhouse for his team. He wanted to decorate it appropriately, and began to search for something suitable. Meanwhile, bitten by the flying bug too, Mr Jullien senior had decided to learn to fly a helicopter – and during a lesson crashed into a lake. Fortunately, he was not seriously hurt, but his misfortune was his son's good luck: Jullien appropriated the resulting wreck of a Robinson 22 to become the first element of his little museum, where it was hung dramatically from the ceiling.

Frédéric Jullien became a renowned pilot – twice French helicopter champion and twice part of the French bronze-medal winning team at the world championships. But at the same time he was pursuing his new-found passion for collecting. It drove him to travel all over the country, seeking out parts of aeroplanes and helicopters, from fuselage to propellers, engines to parachutes, even missiles. He found his favourite piece, a French Djin helicopter built in 1952 (he loves it so much that he often eats his breakfast sitting in it), buried under some straw in a farm, and persuaded the farmer to give it to him. Another favourite is a wheel from a Concorde – a friend of a friend knew an Air France mechanic, who gave him the out-of-order piece of aviation history. He also has the gun and radio equipment from a B17 bomber, the gun of a crashed Dauphin helicopter, and a six-cylinder star-shaped engine. Amazingly, none of the objects in this collection were bought; all were donated, more or less reluctantly, and taken back to contribute to the décor in Jullien's home-cum-clubhouse. He clearly has a great gift of persuasion. The largest object is a 6m (19½ft) high missile that was shown

RIGHT A 6m (19½ft) high missile dominates a corner of the barn, which Jullien uses as an informal aeronautical club. Camouflage netting covers the walls, and his flying trophies are arranged on a thick wooden beam.

LEFT Propellers, posters, wind socks, and aeronautical models mingle informally in Jullien's clubhouse. To him, atmosphere is far more important than pretty arrangements.

ABOVE Jullien did not pay for a single element of his collection. Every item was donated. The models of pilots were presents from friends.

at the Salon Aeronautique du Bouget. "My neigh-bours were very frightened when they saw it arriving on a truck," laughs Jullien. Smaller objects, too, make their contribution to this fascinating collection. They include models of helicopters and planes, large and small; rows of control instruments; and prints, posters (naturally, the flying films *Memphis Belle* and *Top Gun* feature heavily), and photographs. Jullien is proud of his collection of photographs by Michel Lebleux on the subjects of base jumping and para-chuting. Some of these show world-record jumps or extraordinary feats such as an illegal jump from the Tour Montparnasse and 80 women jumping together and linking hands at 2,000m (6,500ft).

This highly personal museum is arranged in an informal, some might even say haphazard, way. It is just like an untidy aircraft hangar, with the missile standing casually in a corner, models resting on the floors, tables, and shelves, and camouflage netting covering the walls. Just for fun, there are a couple of

mannequins, presents from friends, which Jullien dressed up in genuine jumpsuits, helmets, and gog-gles. His competition trophies, too, are on display, perched on top of a wooden beam that makes a great feature in the high-ceilinged space.

The collection means a great deal to him. He freely admits that it is not a classic or even a particu-larly valuable one. But it creates an ambience, a club-like area where his friends, who arrive by all aerial means, can have a good time. They drink whisky leaning on the Concorde wheel and listen to jazz while chatting about aeronautical adventures. But it does not stop there. Typically for Jullien, who "wanted to create an environment where my friends will never forget my invitations", he has gone one step further, and in the background he plays record-ings of the sound of helicopter propellers revolving and old engines revving. His enthusiasm for all things aeronautical truly knows no bounds. "For me, this is just like the best music," he says.

ABOVE Jullien was twice the French helicopter champion, and in his barn a row of control instruments topped by model helicopters makes an unusual display.

"The commonplace artefact is probably more evocative than the more exotic variety."

Robert Opie, London, England
PACKAGING

For Robert Opie, collecting is not just a hobby, or even a passion. It's a mission, a quest, a way of life. Opie's aim is to collect the history of every-thing – or at least, to piece together the jigsaw puzzle of our consumer society, changes that have transformed lives in Britain since the Industrial Revolution. "It's the story of our culture and lifestyle, of travel and transport, design and fashion, communication, leisure, and entertainment, and, of course, shopping. In order to tell this remarkable evolution I need to gather the evidence – examples of the cultural artefacts that illustrate the reality of each development. This is everyday life told through everyday things."

The way in which Opie tells this story is through an ever-evolving, ever-expanding collection that, so far, covers more than half a million of the most typical products of our consumer society past and present. Objects like milk cartons and cereal packets, shampoo bottles and baked bean tins, coffee jars and sugar bags. We may easily take them for granted, but for Opie they are vitally, intensely interesting. "The commonplace artefact is probably more evocative than the more exotic variety," he explains. Thus, within each of a thousand categories, whether toys, comics, kitchen appliances, women's magazines, cameras, record players, or postcards, the focus of the collection is predominantly on the mass-produced items. The evidence from each area represents a thread of a story that makes up the pattern of human life.

Since he was 16, Opie has never thrown away a package, unless it already duplicated one in his collection. The son of eminent collectors, he had since early childhood collected stamps, stones, and coins, and then diecast Lesney Matchbox vehicles. Encouraged by his father to annotate his acquisitions, he began to enter the price and date on each Lesney box; by his teens he was shaping up to be a passionate collector. Seeing that everyone else was collecting stamps, Opie wanted to find subjects which were less well recorded. His philatelic interests turned to postal stationery, stamp booklets, and aerogrammes.

Then came the conversion. Having bought a packet of sweets at Inverness railway station in 1963, he was eating them back at his hotel room when he suddenly realized that the packaging was a little piece of history which,

if he didn't save it, could easily disappear and be forgotten. The 16-year-old schoolboy suddenly saw that packaging was just as worthy of preservation as stamps, coins, or miniature vehicles. From then on the task was to save examples of the packaging and advertising that were around him – the cereal box from the breakfast table or the discarded cigarette packet in the street. His bedroom was soon a little museum.

While taking a business studies course, Opie developed a circuit of local confectioners and tobacconists who he visited every week to pick up display material used in their shop windows. On one occasion he went into a chemist's and bought every brand of toothpaste. Initially, Opie collected just the most common daily brands, but a few years later he began to track down earlier examples of the same products. This led, inexorably, to attempting to trace the history of major brands, including those that have

now long since disappeared – Mazawattee tea, Fry's Five Boys chocolate, Spangles, or Rinso washing powder. By 1975 he had assembled more than enough material to stage a one-man exhibition at London's prestigious Victoria & Albert Museum. Some 3,000 items were selected to fill an entire gallery – bottles, tins, labels, packets, jars, posters, brochures, signs, and so on. The show, called "The Pack Age: A Century of Wrapping it Up", was hugely successful. Opie was encouraged to establish his own museum, one that would tell the story of this consumer revolution.

In 1984 he opened The Museum of Advertising and Packaging in Gloucester, Britain's first such museum. In displays with themes such as ten decades of shopping from the 1880s and Britain during World War II, it featured products that have been stocked by grocers, chemists, sweet shops, pubs, tobacconists, and early supermarkets, their colourful

ABOVE Instead of a picture over his fireplace, Opie has a set of shelves, the contents of which encapsulate the wide variety of packing design. Here are classic examples of major brands, from Oxo to Fry's, Vim to Trex.

RIGHT Using a visible storage system for some of the collection enables quick reference points: "You have to be prepared to tolerate the physical space that these things take up," Opie points out.

labels evoking nostalgia but also tracing social trends, from the development of the car to the emancipation of women, the disappearance of servants to the advent of the marketing industry. In 1993 Opie also put together an exhibition that toured Japan, and another that was at Britain's Chatham Docks for 13 years. Six years later, he opened The Museum of Memories in Wigan, a tour through 150 years of domestic life in Britain.

All the while, however, he was, and still is, writing books, making television appearances, and collecting, collecting, collecting. He spends time at auctions and collectors' fairs, and continues to research his subject in as much depth as he is able. He admits that it runs his life. "I'm studying life and how humans live, so I'm always extending my areas of interest. But often a sample is enough. Take the electric lightbulb. Fortunately, it has hardly changed since the 1880s – that's until the recent arrival of the economy bulb. Knowing what and how much to save of today's material is a constant worry. In theory, you almost have to save examples of everything – in practice, space, time, and money ultimately restrict

the amount." The humble yoghurt pot had arrived just as Opie was beginning to preserve packs for posterity, so this exploding market has received special attention, and now he has nearly 10,000 different examples. At some time in the future, supermarket archaeologists will be able to appreciate the birth of the real fruit yoghurt.

Opie goes to the supermarket most days, looking first for things with which to update his collection. "There are times when I think I am going crazy," he says. "Or that maybe I shouldn't be doing this – but something always makes me keep on going." He still gets a tremendous thrill from a new find, particularly, of course, if it is some historic pack for which he has been searching – he is still looking for an early Heinz baked bean can and a 1940s can of Spam, for example. Not that he often hunts for specific items; rather, he has a mental list of a thousand items which he would like to acquire. "Always finding new things makes it continually exciting," he explains. "As everything connects with everything else, it's the totality that makes it interesting. So where do you stop? You just don't."

"Religious imagery really attracts me. It's where all art comes from."

Billy Shire, Los Angeles, CA, USA
RELIGIOUS IMAGERY

There is perhaps something about the sunny, optimistic climate of California and the brilliance of the light on its landscape that encourages collectors to pursue extravagant, bizarre, and colourful objects. This natural exuberance touched the grand old collectors, such as the great newspaper tycoon William Randolph Hearst, who realized his dream by building his fantasy castle at San Simeon, near Los Angeles. Similarly, Henry Huntington, seemingly a more dour and conservative connoisseur of the old school, having amassed his treasures in a vast mansion at Pasadena, could not resist capping the achievement with a riotously coloured cactus garden and a whole valley landscaped in the Japanese manner, complete with rustic bridges and an extensive tea-pavilion.

Billy Shire, a lifelong collector of unusual and unlikely objects, reveals himself a worthy successor to this great tradition in his house of marvels in Los Angeles. Just as the old collectors would suspend weird and curious creatures from the rafters of their secret studies, so in this latter-day cabinet of wonders a decorative crocodile hangs from the ceiling, illuminated by the eerie glow of contemporary devotional images. In this extraordinary melting pot, treasures from many cultures mingle with more mundane domestic items to create an entirely idiosyncratic mix that is part home and part museum. In his altar-like arrangements, Billy Shire juxtaposes – unselfconsciously, but to considerable effect – African ethnic and tribal carvings, South American crucifixes and saints, and examples of his many and various other collections, from skull ephemera to nutcrackers, swordfish to liquor bottles, 19th-century German folk carvings to Japanese superhero toys.

His predilection for kitsch is inexplicable to Shire, though he feels his eye for craftsmanship was sparked by his father, an artist and carpenter, who built the mid-20th-century house in which Shire was brought up. Shire had always been fascinated by a plaster of Paris skull that his father had made as a student, and it was the theme of skulls and skeletons that constituted his first real foray into collecting – a trip to Mexico in 1975 where he discovered the Day of the Dead ritual and started to buy and bring back related objects. Over the ensuing decades, he steadily collected more, and bigger, pieces, researching their provenance and

RIGHT Shire is fascinated by religious imagery, and one of his larger collections is of crosses and crucifixes. He has more than 200 in sterling silver, and 30 or 40 made from wood, examples of late 19th-century German folk art.

seeking out the artisans who made them, and expanded into collecting all sorts of items from other countries, in South America, Europe, and even the Far East. He formed collections and more collections, and then sub-collections of collections, until he had, literally, thousands of items.

What links together the resulting eclectic mix is the strong visual appeal of each piece, whether it be the patina of his father's skull carving – still an icon for Shire – or the hand-painted and sequinned Voudoun flags of which he has about 40. "I'm not religious at all, but religious imagery really attracts me," he explains. "It's where all art comes from. And I'm also really into ritual objects – we're talking primordial." Shire's collections were the basis for the gallery which he opened in 1986, La Luz de Jesus, a

pop culture supermarket which he describes as oriented to karmic hot rod pin-up California culture and which has earned him the sobriquet the Peggy Guggenheim of Lowbrow.

Now, however, Shire restricts his collecting mainly to art, which means only one piece from each show at the gallery. "It's a little preposterous to have so much stuff," he admits. "These days my collecting isn't so much of a mania as it was – I'm kind of over that. When I was in the middle of it all, from the late 1970s to the 90s, it was a lifestyle; it was all about the hunt, going to the flea markets, the art fairs, the antique toy shows, the ethnographic art shows. I still like to look at it all, but unlike some people, I'm not so attached to it that I couldn't sell it if I had to."

ABOVE In a sitting room familiar domestic objects and the outright bizarre co-exist happily, grouped around a chimneypiece flanked by eccentric, asymmetric twisted columns.

RIGHT A corner of the room is inhabited by a group of figures that includes brightly coloured ethnic carvings, an advertisement in the form of an oversize bug, and a medical model that contrives to reveal the internal organs while nevertheless remaining decorously swathed.

NEXT PAGE Shire's collection spills out into his garage, which is hung with Mexican, Bolivian, and African masks. The Tree of Death on the left is made of painted clay. On the right is a wooden pony from Guatemala, part of a fake backdrop that belonged to an itinerant photographer.

"I started with just one and kept thinking how vivid it looked, like a tiny person."

Eric & Jutta Meletta, Munich, Germany
MANNEQUINS

Eric and Jutta Meletta's Munich apartment is full of life. Not because they collect cats, dogs, birds, or even beetles, though. No. They collect, among other things, antique wooden mannequins – the little articulated figures used by artists as models for their work, particularly in the 18th century, when aristocratic subjects were far too busy to pose for anything other than their faces. The mannequins were made large and small, with more or less detail, in exact proportion to the human body, and with limbs (sometimes even fingers) that could be manoeuvred into an array of poses to look as real as possible.

The Melettas love their little people, which they regularly reposition in varying stances all around the apartment. "We move them around, sometimes in the library, sometimes on the window seat," says Eric Meletta. "I started with just one which I had sitting in my library, and I kept looking at it and thinking how vivid it looked. Not dead, like a book or a work of art, but like a tiny person. They look so unusual, and every day you can have something different."

Over the course of 20 years Eric Meletta, a dealer in antique English and French furniture, has collected 13 or 14 of these mannequins, choice examples all dating back to the 18th or 19th centuries, though he has found it increasingly difficult to find good pieces in recent years. Fortunately, he has two other collections to which he can turn his attention. One of them is of *veilleuses*, or bedroom lamps, made to give a gentle glow in a bedroom and to be left on while the occupant slept. Meletta has about 20, all from around 1900 and thus in the Art Nouveau style. Made of glass, they are cut or moulded, some abstract, some shaped as figures, some relatively plain, and others highly decorated. He has displayed them in an orderly fashion in his library where, as he says, they give a wonderful atmosphere.

His other collection is of souvenir objects from the Grand Tour, that unique phenomenon of the 18th and 19th centuries in which well-off young men would, as part of their educational process, be guided around Europe – especially Italy and Greece – learning about art, culture, and politics. When they came across an artefact too large to carry home as a memento, an arch, column, or coliseum,

RIGHT This delightful wooden mannequin dates to the 19th century. The Melettas love to move their little people around the apartment, posing them in different stances.

ABOVE On a sideboard in the library, the Melettas display their collection of souvenirs of the Grand Tour – replicas of famous monuments, brought back from Greece or Italy in the late 18th and early 19th centuries.

RIGHT The mannequins are gathered on a ladder in a range of poses. The top one, which is 1.4m (4½ft) tall, is very early, and has articulated fingers.

perhaps, they instead purchased a small-scale souvenir (early examples of the tourist trade), many of which were made with great skill and artistry. This, in fact, is where Meletta started his collecting. When he was about 25 he came across a pair of silver-plated candlesticks in a flea market in Paris, reeded columns with a beautifully worked capital. "They were a wonderful model and they fascinated me," he remembers. The collection, over the next 30 or so years, grew from there, including replicas of columns in Alexandria, arches in Rome, and obelisks in France.

Again, the Meletta's 35 or 40 Grand Tour souvenirs are displayed with art and precision. Their apartment, though not entirely designed around their objects, was certainly created with them in mind. The walls were washed with layers of sienna yellow paint to give a consistent, attractive, and appropriate backdrop to the pieces, and sideboards placed so the items could be placed on top of them. Plug sockets were ranged along the walls so that the *veilleuses* could all be switched on at once, and subtle lighting installed to make the most, not just of the inanimate objects, but also of visitors to the apartment as well. "Lighting is very important, says Eric Meletta. I'm very sensitive to it, and we made sure that it would be really flattering." Without doubt, this is a setting that does maximum justice to a choice collection of intriguing objects, but also to the way in which the Melettas live. Truly a case of art and life mingling with absolute ease.

ABOVE The veilleuses give a beautiful glow, especially against the carefully chosen paintwork. The apartment was not exactly designed around the collection, but everything was integrated so that the Meletta's pieces would be shown to best advantage.

"That's the joy of collecting, to stimulate the young and the old. But it's hard work."

Brian Thompson, Staplehurst, Kent, England
AGRICULTURAL EQUIPMENT

Brattle Farm is a working farm, with 500 acres sown with winter wheat, rape, and beans. But it is also a museum where, alongside the shiny new equipment that modern agriculture requires, vintage farm vehicles, machinery, and tools are displayed, as well as bygones demonstrating the rural life, craft, and trade of England in the last two centuries.

The collection – which numbers thousands of objects both familiar and esoteric – has been built up by the farm's owner, Brian Thompson, a driven collector. He started out as a small boy with stamps and birds' eggs, and progressed in the early 1970s, after a couple of decades of running the farm, to vintage cars, the first of which was a 1928 Austin Heavy 12/4, with two seats and a "dicky", or "mother-in-law" seat, at the back. Thompson soon found that vintage wrecks were plentiful and cheap, and spent the winters – after the arable land was safely sown with wheat – restoring his finds, each one taking two or three years.

When Thompson decided to give up farming dairy cows and chickens, he had at his disposal the drying floor of the farm's oasthouse. So he began bidding for lots of old iron in the farm sales where he often came across his old cars. He was fascinated by the inventiveness shown by hand-forged implements and could not bear the thought that hundreds of years of farming were being thrown away. He later gave up pigs, too, after heavy losses, which freed up the ground floor of the oasthouse for a new collection: heavy farm machinery. He liked to keep things local, with manufacturers such as Tetts of Faversham, and Weeks and Drake & Fletcher of Maidstone. Holidays were spent visiting fellow enthusiasts and their collections. The museum opened to the public in 1975.

Next came tractors, which to Thompson's delight did not need upholstery or hoods, and which showed even more clearly the leaps of imagination in their designs. He bought, moved, and rebuilt a barn in which to display them. But in May 1984 disaster struck. A fire, which had started in baled straw, destroyed all the farm buildings except the house and a few prefabs (including the one in which the vintage cars were housed). Huge efforts had to be made to continue. The oasthouse was rebuilt, and the barn and small sheds replaced by modern

RIGHT At one end of the vast ground floor of the oasthouse is the blacksmith's display. Though there is a great deal of it, all the old equipment at Brattle Farm Museum is arranged in groups and neatly labelled.

structures. Thompson bought replacement tractors – a 1918 Titan and a 1917 Waterloo Boy, both from Ireland, which escaped the scrap collections of World War II. From Sark came the wreck of a 1918 International Junior, once the only vehicle on the island, sawn into two to fit into a fishing boat's hold. Closer to home, in a nearby Kentish village, he found a 1914 Weeks Dungey, a true rarity and one of the very earliest British tractors ever produced.

And so it went on. As well as the cars, the tractors, and the heavy machinery, Brattle Farm is home to many smaller collections, assembled by Thompson and his wife Anita, a keen local historian, over the years. There are displays showing a dairy, a blacksmith's, a wheelwright's and a carpenter's shop, a kitchen, and a laundry. There is veterinary and sheepshearing equipment. There are exhibits related to hop and fruit growing, to bee keeping, to

horse care, to warfare, to brick- and tile-making, and to wood cutting. There are lawnmowers, bicycles, locks, printing blocks, cider presses, coal hole covers, ration books, medals, taps, cameras, and tin openers. From a clod crusher to a huvvering fork, one can see the entire agricultural history of this corner of Kent here. Neatly labelled, everything is displayed in densely packed groups, sometimes so crowded there is barely room to squeeze between them. "The museum is filled with things that everyone threw out, found in Uncle's Jack's garden shed, or Aunt Maisie's bathroom cupboard, or in the barn that is now an expensive country house," says Brian. "Older people always say: 'I've got one of those!', while children gaze with fascinated horror at the two-holer loo or the water pump in the kitchen. That's the joy of collecting, to stimulate the young and the old. But it's hard work."

LEFT The tractors. Thompson travelled far and wide to collect examples from the early 20th century, including some rare models such as a 1914 Weeks Dungey.

ABOVE A dummy of a farmer sewing corn greets visitors to the oasthouse. Next to him is a display of vintage food containers.

RIGHT In the wood cutting area, antique saws are hung on the walls like works of art.

"I load and unload my figures, symbolically and sentimentally, with thoughts and desires."

Horst Antes, Berlin, Germany
KACHINA FIGURES

RIGHT Antes' collection of kachina figures is believed to be the largest in the world, with the greatest variety of models. Usually about 30cm (12in) high, these wooden figures are vividly painted.

Artists have frequently been drawn to tribal cultures, finding inspiration and influence in the unknown, in what to them seemed primitive and different. With Pablo Picasso and Georges Braque, famously, it was African sculpture, which they admired and collected, displayed in their studios, and often used as models; with other European artists, included Max Ernst, André Breton, Marcel Duchamp, and Emil Nolde, it was the less well-known culture of the Pueblo Indians, based in the South-West of North America.

The Pueblo traditions, common to the Hopi, Zuni, and Navajo tribes, have withstood centuries of change, of incursions by zealous Spanish missionaries, and by the "civilizing" forces of US culture. The strength of their culture is based around a belief system that ignores conventional time lines and the recording of experiences, but instead concentrates on a view of the world as an harmonious relationship between gods, humans, and other beings and forces. Religious ceremonies are used to maintain this precious balance – ceremonies in which spirits of the tribal ancestors, called kachina, are personified by dancers, always male, dressed in elaborate masks and costumes in order to represent the hundreds of different spirits. Hopi kachina signify plants, animals, insects, human qualities, the creative force of the sun, and even death. Some are demons who frighten children into behaving properly, some are profane or amusing; most are clan ancestors and benevolent beings. As messengers, they accept gifts and prayers for health, fertility, and rain and carry them back to the gods. Their role as rainmakers is especially important to the Hopi, who farm in the high, arid deserts of north-eastern Arizona.

As bearers of a small portion of the power of the kachina, the small wooden figures that are carved by the tribesmen are hugely important. Made from the root of the cottonwood tree, about 30cm (12in) high and boldly painted in vivid colours, they are effigies of the kachina, traditionally given to infants, girls, and young women as educational tools, to instruct them about the spirits, and as good luck talismans; they were, in particular, intended to guarantee that the girl would grow up in good health and bear strong children later in life. When received, they are greatly respected and treated with veneration.

The carved kachina figures are effigies of the spirits of Hopi tribal ancestors, and as such they are believed to bear a small portion of the power of the spirits. They can be war-like and fearsome, or simple representations of plants, animals, or insects.

At the end of the 19th century, the kachina dolls were discovered with enthusiasm by early tourists and anthropologists, and the Hopi men started to produce them to sell. In time, they became recognized as a significant form of tribal art. Encouraged by white collectors, the art of carving kachina (or *tihu*, as they are called by the Hopi) developed during the 20th century, from flat figures to modern, moveable ones which are full of impact.

In the mid 20th century the Surrealist artist Max Ernst, who emigrated to the USA in 1941, became fascinated by these dolls and established a large collection of them. More recently, fellow German painter, sculptor and printmaker Horst Antes, a significant 20th-century artist and principal representative of the Fantastic Realism movement, has followed his example, though he has developed his interest even further and put together a collection that numbers more than 700 kachina figures and is

believed to be the largest in the world, with probably the greatest diversity of models. A true obsessive, Antes also collects other objects, including feather works by South American Indians, toy robots, votives, packaging, and children's books. It is the kachina, however, which remain his primary focus.

Although he studied art, Antes was always drawn towards anthropology, and became interested in the culture of the Hopi, Zuni, and Navajo in the late 1950s. In 1961 he bought his first kachina figure in Paris, enticed by its shape, its carving, and its colours. From there he never looked back. Not one to do things by halves, he collected widely, intensely, and systematically, establishing relationships with other collectors, visiting the reservations of south-west America and putting together a library of material around the topic. He researched the culture and artistic expressions of the Pueblo Indians, campaigned for the freedom of the Hopi people and,

eventually, became deputy chair of the Future for Children charity, which promotes sponsorship for Hopi, Zuni, and Navajo children. Antes was the only non-Hopi participant in the 1981 kachina exhibition Spirit of Life at the American Museum of Natural History in New York, which was accompanied by a book about his collection.

Antes' intention was never simply to use the kachina figures as inspiration, but rather to study them, to assemble an archive of form, and to try to understand their coded messages which, for the Indians, bring order into the world. He feels a spiritual bond with the Indians, and his own work is intimately bound up with his lifetime of collecting kachina in a way that is inextricable and, probably, unavoidable. Both show evidence of a bold use of colour and of the invention of a specific artistic figure: in Antes' case, he invented a representative of the human being that he called a *Kopfüssler*, or

"head-footer", a figure represented by a huge head, eye, or foot, but never a body. His work is a series of attempts to discover myth in order to explain the world – rather as the kachina stand for individual spirits but also for the community and for all surrounding elements, and thus explain the world to the Hopi and other Indians. For Antes, the roots of artistic expression are in religion, and his own art is based around the premise of grasping the idea of the human. "I load and unload my figures," he says. "Symbolically, sentimentally, organically, historically, I fill them and empty them with references, gestures, thoughts, speculations, desires, and anxieties." The kachina, similarly, both dolls and dancers, are loaded with references. Picasso once said that the African sculptures that stood dotted around his studio were testimonies rather than models. The same could be said of the relationship between Antes and his collection.

ABOVE Koshari kachina are both sacred and profane. They are amusing, but do not set a good example of human behaviour and are often depicted with a watermelon to indicate gluttony.

"I bought a third machine, then a fourth. This is what happens to collectors!"

Jean-Claude Baudot, Paris, France
SLOT MACHINES

The millions who chance their luck in the casinos of Las Vegas every year probably never spare a thought for Heron of Alexandria. But without Heron, who knows whether the enticing bright lights of this desert city would exist? For Heron, in his book *Pneumatic*, of about 200BC, described with uncanny accuracy the form and mechanism of the first-known automatic vending machine. Invented for priests, it was in the shape of a vase, with a slit in the top for a coin, and dispensed holy water whenever a coin was dropped onto a lever inside. Eureka! Only an inch away from the modern slot machine.

In the centuries that followed, kings and emperors commissioned specially designed automatic games from artists and craftsmen. Leonardo da Vinci himself built three slot machines. But it was not until the mid 19th century that such ingenious inventions started to make an impression upon ordinary people. The first coin-operated slot machine in the USA was built in 1839 to sell cigarette papers, while in 1857 an English patent was taken out for an automatic postage stamp machine, and ten years later in France and Germany similar devices appeared selling cigarettes and handkerchiefs. By the beginning of the 20th century, mass production of automatic machines was in full swing – and the slot machine of the *belle époque* became the blank canvas for any and every trend in popular art. Wooden or metal boxes were sculpted into elaborate shapes with mouldings or painted or printed panels, all the while disguising ever more complex and intricately engineered workings.

Jean-Claude Baudot became fascinated by slot machines when he was a conscript in the French army. Looking for a one-armed bandit just for the fun of it, he came across a crazy 1895 French machine featuring a clown and propelling balls in the Paris flea market of Clignancourt. He could not resist. "Later, still at the flea market, I found another, similar, machine," he says. "It had a wheel which turned a little person – Josephine Baker. Then I bought a third machine, then a fourth. This is what happens to collectors!"

Baudot didn't stop. After 40 years he has amassed some 600 machines of all types – shooting galleries, test-your-strength machines, pinballs, one-armed bandits, vending machines, and a wealth of games, examples of almost all the

RIGHT **From The Little Stockbroker to the Clever Dog, horse racing to roulette, games of chance are Baudot's passion and pride and joy. They are gorgeously decorated in a range of styles, and make a wonderful display.**

LEFT Ornamented with Fortuna, the goddess of chance, this railway game is one of a type popular in casinos in the 19th century. An early version of a roulette wheel, the train travels round, and stops to indicate the winning number.

ABOVE In 40 years, Baudot has collected some extraordinary and unusual pieces from around the world. The silver, robot-like figure on the left is the Carpentier, a rare 1920s Cubist design. Next to him is an American Tug O War of 1904, while the ghoulish French *L'heure de votre mort* (the hour of your death), is the only one of its kind known, dating from around 1900.

finest machines produced by the notable manufacturers in America, England, France, and Germany. It is one of the world's most important collections of its kind – his aim is to open a public museum for it – but it is also great fun, including such wonders as the Electric Shock Pig, a life-sized porker whose eyes light up while a dial on its belly registers electric current; the Cluck Hen and the Elephant, which dispense chocolate; and the Carpentier, a robot-like French Cubist machine with two fighters, the only such model known.

Baudot is clearly a man who throws himself enthusiastically into whatever he does. In 1958, with Jacques Séguéla, he completed the first ever round-the-world trip in a Citroen 2CV, crossing six seas, five continents, eight deserts, and five moun-

tain ranges, on one occasion using a banana to avert a potential disaster with the gearbox. He has also collected 3,000 antique toys, dolls, and games, and opened a museum for them at Canet-en-Roussillon, in the South of France. For his 1,700 items of Father Christmas memorabilia he would also like to open a museum somewhere, and alongside it he plans to erect a statue of Santa. Being Jean-Claude Baudot, however, his statue would be no ordinary effigy. In what is typical of his effusive and infectious sense of fun, his statue would be huge, larger than the Statue of Liberty, capturing the idea of childhood and the family. For now, Baudot is busy lobbying town councils around the country to get his idea off the ground. And, knowing him, it will not be long before he succeeds.

ABOVE In the living room of Baudot's farmhouse in the South of France he keeps a jukebox and a one-armed bandit. On the table is displayed an impressive collection of lottery machines.

avant garde and chic

SOME OF THE MOST EMINENT COLLECTIONS OF THE 21ST CENTURY ARE OF MODERN AND AVANT-GARDE ART. IN THIS CHAPTER WE REVEAL AN EXTRAORDINARY RANGE OF PAINTINGS, SCULPTURE, INSTALLATIONS, AND OTHER WORKS FROM AROUND THE WORLD, EACH OF THEM DISPLAYED WITH PANACHE, VERVE, AND UNERRING STYLE.

> *"Collecting is obsessive. You are always looking for the next great discovery."*

Martin Margulies, Miami, FL, USA
MODERN ART

From the businesslike, down-to-earth world of real estate to the heady, esoteric heights of contemporary art may seem like a giant leap, but for one man, Martin Z Margulies, it has been a small step, as straightforward for him as buying a plot of land or selling a million dollar condominium. He tells the story of his move from South Florida property developer to art collector (and donor) extraordinaire in a typically humorous and self-deprecating way: "I used to just love girls when I was younger. I was a businessman for years, and I thought it would be fun to have a different interest in my life. Collecting contemporary art just seemed to fit the bill. I met a few people and one thing just seemed to lead to another. Initially, I had an advisor, but sadly we parted ways. Now I have a board of directors – my children, aged 14, 16, 22, and 24 years old."

In fact, Margulies, totally self-taught, has developed a knowledge and expertise that could rival that of many an art professional. It was not always that way, however. He admits that when he first started he was almost completely ignorant. "I really didn't know what I was doing," he says. "But I started to develop a little more learning, and became more informed. Unfortunately, the more I got into it, the more I realized how much I didn't know." These, days, his collection is not only extensive, numbering around 3,500 pieces, but also particularly fine – albeit sometimes unusual, daring, even shocking. Margulies enjoys pieces that provoke thought and ask questions, such as Gilles Barbier's life-sized elderly superheroes, and Ernesto Neto's pendant clusters of fabric filled with fragrant spices. "We need more questions," he says. The collection includes photography, video, installation, painting, and sculpture, and is based at three sites: at his home in Key Biscayne; in a converted 10,000m (35,000ft) warehouse in downtown Miami, which is open to the public and for student and group tours; and in a sculpture park at the Florida International University. In the latter space many examples of monumental sculpture, including classic 1960s and 1970s works by Richard Serra and Sol Lewitt, are on long-term loan, while at his private penthouse he keeps blue-chip works by such well-known names as Mark Rothko and Jasper Johns.

RIGHT The large open spaces of The Warehouse lend themselves to large-scale installations. In Gilles Barbier's *L'Hospice*, six wax figures, both shocking and amusing, depict elderly superheroes waiting for treatment.

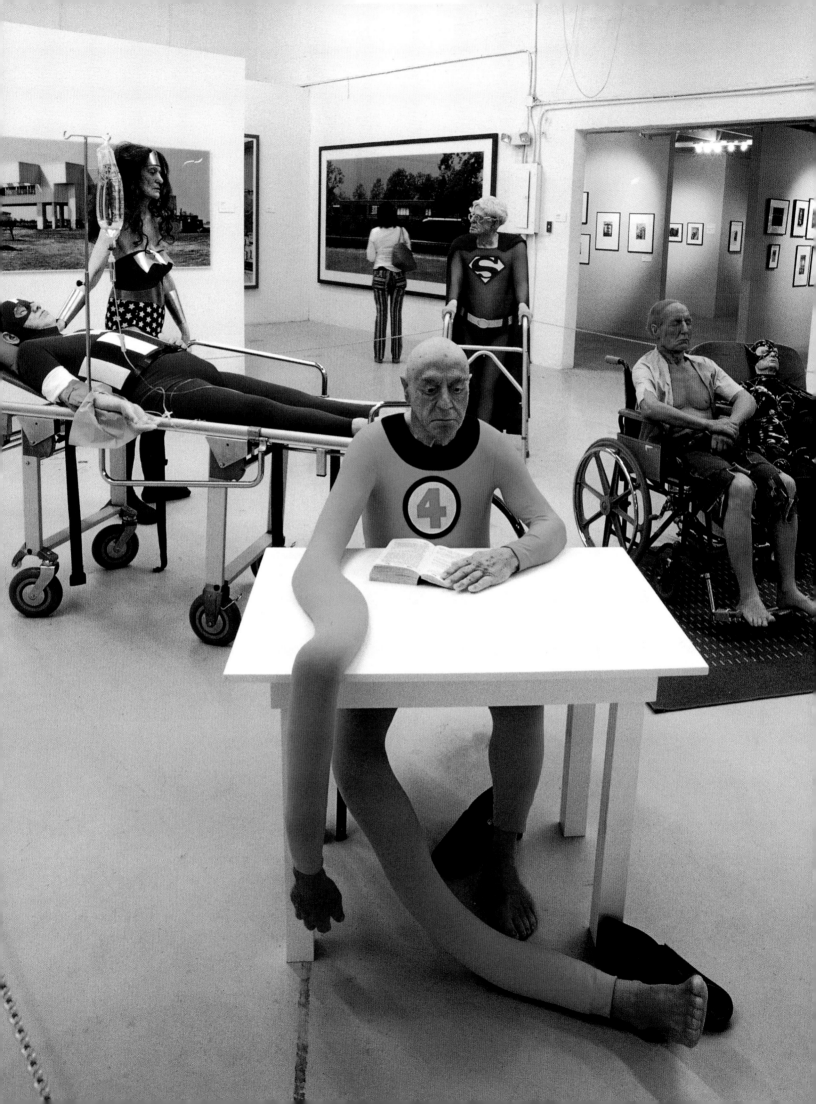

The Warehouse, which was opened in 1999, has an extensive collection of recently acquired art. The photography collection, which includes seminal works from 1910 to the present, represents major shifts in photographic art, from Social Realism and American Humanist to European Modernism and Conceptualism. Installation art, ideally suited to The Warehouse, with its vast, open spaces and 6m (20ft) ceilings, includes works by internationally prominent artists such as Ernesto Neto, Ann Sofi Siden, and Joseph Kosuth. The video art is compelling, challenging, and unquestionably contemporary, including pieces by Peter Friedl, Vanessa Beecroft, and Andrea Bowers, while the sculpture collection is well known for its international names, from Anthony Gormley and Anish Kapoor to Dan Flavin and Tony Cragg.

For Margulies, one of the greatest pleasures has been to open The Warehouse and enjoy the educational experience that it offers to so many young people. "If more young people got involved in art the world would probably be a better place," he says. "Instead of learning how to make bombs, people would have a more creative aspect to their lives." On the other hand, he jokes that collecting is "a very wonderful, useless activity, though it's also extremely satisfying and enjoyable. It is obsessive; you are always looking for that great discovery." Even though he has been collecting for decades, he constantly finds surprising new aspects to much-loved, familiar works, and is determined to continue his passion. Like all true collectors, new acquisitions are never far from his mind, and wherever he goes he visits galleries and looks at art, seeking pieces which both elicit a personal response and which will fit into the oeuvre. "Because when you have a collection it becomes a body of work, a rhythm, and it must be cohesive." At the end of the day this is a pursuit that is not about business, or money, or even education. "There are no goals, he says. The whole point is just to have fun."

LEFT There is no doubt that Margulies' contemporary art collection is at the cutting edge. This piece by the renowned Brazilian sculptor Ernesto Neto is called *É Ô Bischo!*, and is made from Lycra tulle and spices.

ABOVE Margulies' aim is to educate and stimulate. This piece, a kind of surreal doll's house, is Thomas Hirschhorn's *La Maison Commune*, of 2001.

RIGHT In the foreground is Christine Borland's *The Dead Teach the Living*, a series of plaster busts on concrete bases, while in the background can be seen Jason Rhoades' *One Half Thousand Gallon Wall*, made up of 400 one-gallon jars on shelving.

"There has never been a financial side to my collecting. I just need stuff."

Jean Pigozzi, USA
AFRICAN ART

For Jean Pigozzi, collecting is a disease. "It's dangerous," he laughs. "But don't worry – it's not contagious." Pigozzi has suffered from the disease since childhood and has never rid himself of it; he knows that it's a chronic condition that will always afflict him.

The millionaire venture capitalist and photographer is best known for his collection of contemporary African art, which is the most important and extensive in the world, encompassing many artists whom Pigozzi himself helped bring to the public attention. He caught this particular bug in July 1989, when visiting the exhibition "Les Magiciens de la Terre" at the Centre Georges Pompidou in Paris. He was captivated by the vibrancy and innovation of the African art on show there, and enlisted the help of one of the co-curators, André Magnin, to help him start his own collection. They travelled through West Africa in search of art, sculpture, and photography, and amassed a range of pieces, to which Pigozzi has added over the years in what he calls "my ultimate obsession".

But Pigozzi, who began as a child with the traditional collector's training ground of stamp collecting, is also interested in the lowbrow and the kitsch. In fact, it's harder to say what he is not interested in. "There has never been a financial side to my collecting," he says. "I just need stuff. It might be plastic cars, it might be black stones from a beach, or Barbies in bizarre outfits, or funny wooden toys. Last week I was in Russia, and I started a collection of those little dolls that sit inside each other. I start new collections all the time." Between what Pigozzi calls his "junk" and the more eminent collections – of art, of work by the American photographer Weegee, of furniture by Ettore Sottsass – there are all sorts of other collections, among them paintings of UFOs, Mexican figurines, what he describes as "bad pottery from the 1960s from the South of France", which he is amazed to find is now hugely fashionable, and "bad paintings, by what are known as 'peintres de dimanches', or Sunday painters". He has thousands of things ("I could never move," he laughs), and loves them all. What he loves most, however, is a living, breathing collection. "Oh yes, I also collect dogs. I have five weimaraners," he explains. "I have always been a collector and I always will be a collector. You could definitely say that I am not a minimalist."

RIGHT Pigozzi keeps a growing collection of odd pieces on the dining table in his apartment. "This is just a visual mess," says Pigozzi. "It's just junk that I have found, brought back from trips, or that's been given to me." He is unconcerned about display, and when he has a dinner party simply pushes it all to the middle of the table.

ABOVE A mask made from metal, plastic, and junk, by African artist Dak Pogan, is displayed on a wall in Pigozzi's apartment.

RIGHT Pigozzi bought 16 of these African beaded chairs in New York. He loves their vivid colours and bold patterns.

RIGHT Small plastic toys and robots are interspersed with wooden sculptures by Georges Lilanga, against a background of a large painting by Francesco Clemente.

"I am an editor and supplier of raw materials, and the public makes of them what they will."

Mitchell Wolfson, Jr, Miami, FL, USA
CULTURAL COLLECTOR

Mitchell Wolfson, Jr, insists that he is definitely not a collector. "I don't collect, I conserve. I am a preservationist, a missionary. It looks like I'm a hoarder, but actually I'm a hunter-gatherer. I care about objects, but I have no sense of possession. If I love something, I buy it, but I stop loving it once it's acquired." Yet his collecting (for want of a better word) has been determined and consistent, an occupation which has driven him since childhood and which has resulted in a collection that is internationally renowned.

Wolfson, a native Floridian, was heir to a family fortune acquired in the business of constructing movie theatres during the golden age of Hollywood. The relationship between what appears to be frivolous and ephemeral and the shaping of culture would prove significant in informing Wolfson's collector's eye. He was educated at Princeton, where he studied European civilization, and at the Johns Hopkins School of Advanced International Studies. He was always interested in both modern history and art and design, and his collecting reflected an unusual take on how these disciplines related: "It seems to me that the art object is an integral part of the person and the era that produced it, so by studying the art object one can understand more about human behaviour and motivation. I believe that how man expresses himself is more honest and forceful than the sword. I am interested in the language of objects." Wolfson adds that his collection is, in this sense, a reflection of himself, an autobiographical account of his philosophical considerations, concerns, and ambitions, in concrete form.

Although elements of Wolfson's collection can be found at his two offices and his five apartments, the vast majority of it – more than 70,000 objects – is housed at the Wolfsonian-FIU, a seven-storey museum in Miami's South Beach district. The museum was opened in 1995 and its contents donated to Florida International University in 1997. Worth around $75 million at the time, it was one of the USA's largest-ever philanthropic gifts. Wolfson had always intended the collection to be seen by the public and to be an educational resource, to provoke thought and discussion.

The Wolfsonian-FIU's mission, like that of Wolfson himself, is to explore the ideological meanings of decorative objects in diverse forms including

RIGHT In Wolfson's apartment in Miami, a mechanical chair by Cynthia Wynn made of automotive parts dominates one room. On the wall are a pair of bronzes by Mario Moschi which came from the Fiat showroom in Italy, while in the background is a T-bird breakfast table by Dakota Jackson.

ABOVE **Behind a beautifully detailed model steam engine hangs a fascinating Polish woven triptych featuring Nazi iconography, which Wolfson commissioned specially.**

furniture, posters, paintings, sculpture, costumes, textiles, architectural models, books, brochures, and souvenirs. Among its major strengths are Depression-era prints and mural studies by Works Projects Administration artists, items from the British Arts and Crafts movement, examples of turn-of-the-20th century German graphic design, and materials from Nazi Germany and the Soviet Union. It focuses on the period 1885–1945, the crucial time that saw the development of modernity and that brought enormous, sweeping changes in technology, politics, culture, and society. The museum's exhibitions examine the social framework of art and the ways in which design shapes and reflects human experience. It does not shrink from the provocative, displaying propaganda in all its forms including, for example, an

unnerving juxtaposition of eagles used as icons on a Nazi plaque, a fascist flag, and a US poster.

For Wolfson, the value of an object is not what it is worth in monetary terms, nor even in how attractive it is. Instead, it lies in what it can tell us about the culture that produced it, and this is what keeps him collecting. "To say that I have travelled far and wide would be an understatement," he says. "It's been a constant of my existence. This is all part of a narrative, and I look to pieces to fulfil their role in the narrative. Each piece has to complete a phrase, a sentence, or a chapter. The theme and the image count more than the truth or the beauty. However, at the end of the day, I am an editor and a supplier of raw materials, and the curators and the public make of them what they will."

LEFT The metal cup on the left came from India and is typical of some of the smaller pieces that Wolfson gathers on his travels. On the right is a Nazi propaganda piece.

NEXT PAGE Intriguingly, Wolfson also has the second-largest collection of keys in the world. He has collected hotel keys since adolescence and now has about 5,000. "They remind me of where I have been," he says.

ABOVE In Wolfson's guest apartment sits a wooden train repair bike, and on the wall is a modern Nicaraguan tapestry. While continuing to collect pieces for his 1885–1945 collection, Wolfson also admires and occasionally buys contemporary craft, too.

"To hang a frame without a picture – a pure object – that is the greatest possible luxury."

Olaf Lemke, Berlin, Germany
ANTIQUE FRAMES

Olaf Lemke is one of a diminishing number of antique picture frame restorers and dealers. Every year, fine examples of handmade frames become harder and harder to find, while the cost of careful restoration – which can take months of painstaking work – rises to ever higher levels. Thus both the art of collecting and the necessities of business become more challenging. For now, however, Lemke has one of the finest collections of antique frames anywhere, some 2,400 of them, dating from the 15th to the early 19th centuries. They are displayed as works of art in their own right against the walls of his gallery in Berlin.

There is no doubt that Lemke is an expert and connoisseur. Having trained as a gilder with the firms Sprengel and Bruno Wormuth in Berlin in the late 1950s, he spent a year as a journeyman, then answered an advertisement from a London firm, FA Pollak, which made replicas of antique frames. The firm of a Jewish emigrant who had fled from the Nazis, their work was so good that customers could rarely tell the copy from the original. After three years of this demanding apprenticeship, Lemke returned to Berlin where he was offered co-ownership of a firm that restored furniture, frames, and sculptures. Here he stayed for ten years, before eventually setting up his frame business, Antike Rahmen, in 1970.

The fascination with frames began in the 1960s, when Lemke would buy the occasional interesting frame from an art dealer if he happened to come across one. Then Georg Sprengel, now a friend, mentioned to him that it was possible to find good frames in Spain. In 1969 Lemke and his wife Johanna took a holiday in Ibiza, and decided to visit the Rastro market in Madrid. "We could hardly believe what we saw," recalls Lemke. "Absolutely magnificent frames from the 16th, 17th, and 18th centuries containing third-grade pictures and prints. We were intoxicated, and started to buy without knowing one word of Spanish. But we had 20,000 German marks in our pockets, and the language of money always works miracles. The result: 120 fantastic frames, half of them from the 16th century, the rest 17th and 18th century. We were terribly excited, and the Spaniards were pleased to get money for what they called these old pieces of wood."

RIGHT Even the corridors of Lemke's gallery are adorned with beautiful frames. These are 17th century, mostly from Holland and Italy, some gilded, some finished with old, foxed mirror, and some relatively plain.

ABOVE Surviving frames such as these examples from the 17th century were often produced for the Church, and as such are highly ornate. Lemke goes to great lengths to restore them accurately and sensitively.

RIGHT Lemke sometimes holds dinner parties in the atmospheric 17th-century Room, which boasts fabulous cornicing and antique chandeliers. The room on the right contains frames from the 15th and 16th centuries.

On the strength of this purchase, Lemke was able to start his own business. And for years he continued to travel to Spain, where there was stock of good-quality Dutch, Italian, German, and French frames at, until quite recently, reasonable prices. He bought what he could get, building a collection haphazardly, though always with a view to selling rather than keeping pieces. "Inwardly one has to distance oneself from things. So once a frame is hung on the walls of my shop, it is meant to be sold. Otherwise you would be a bad dealer and businessman."

The value of old frames is not appreciated by everyone. Picasso used antique frames for his collection of paintings, and back in the days when art collections were owned by princes, frames were once as highly valued as their contents, but modern collectors have often demonstrated their pride in a

purchase by giving it a new frame, while museums have replaced ornate old frames with simple modern ones. Even worse, for Lemke, however, are the art historians who want to alter a frame in order to fit a particular painting. "You don't cut ten centimetres off a painting or a piece of furniture," he points out. But they will insist on altering the original proportions of a frame, its carvings, embossings and grain, which is an outrage he tries to avoid at all costs.

Yet Lemke is philosophical about his frames. I have Jewish friends who survived the Holocaust. All their belongings vanished and they were humiliated beyond description. Whatever I own only belongs to me for a limited period of time and my collection is not essential for my life. To hang a frame without a picture on the wall – a pure object – that is the ultimate luxury. The greatest possible luxury."

ABOVE **Frames from the 18th century are shown with antique furniture – and the personal touch of a few family photographs tucked into a corner or two.**

"When you see an object you are familiar with so transformed it really takes you by surprise."

Rosamond Purcell, Boston, MA, USA

WEATHERED, FOUND OBJECTS

Photographer, artist, sculptor, writer, and compulsive collector, Rosamond Purcell cherishes things for what they may become. Man-made, perfect and brand new are anathema; for her, it is the effects of the weather and the passage of time, the wear and deterioration that fascinate. "I admit to an attraction to and tolerance for the most friable things," she says. "Patina, rust, and almost total evaporation do not distress me. Cracks, warping, holes, and shards add unpredictable and welcome complexity to many objects, turning the tedium of manufactured clones into singularities."

It was more than 20 years ago that Purcell, while teaching a photography workshop, discovered an extraordinary junkyard, owned by one William Buckminster. As she recounts: "On a visit to Owls Head, Maine, in the 1980s, I came across 11 acres covered by two centuries' worth of weathered, formerly useful objects. Every few months since, I have made a pilgrimage to this site, which became my single most important source of materials. On her first trip she found a couple of seminal objects, both of which were, and still are, a source of inspiration. The first was what she calls a "book-nest", a pair of books fused together by the elements and adopted by a family of mice as a nest. The title of the top book is *Flying Hostesses of the Air* – so this is literally pulp fiction," says Purcell. "There are so many layers of meaning in it." The second object was a "reduced" typewriter, rusted down to the hammers so that it resembled a fossil or a sea urchin. "These objects triggered my whole desire to explore, dig out, and possess artefacts that had been affected by the natural process," explains Purcell.

Since that time, Purcell has gathered a vast number and range of such objects in her studio at Somerville, Massachusetts, a studio that serves as a constantly changing and evolving installation. The objects can be seen in a new context, redefined according to the rules of Purcell's alternative value-system. Among the thousands of specimens are farm machinery, garden tools, old windows, broken chairs, ladders, anchors, tree roots, light fixtures, an entire library of ruined books, and a wall made from patinated scrap metal. "Out on the sharp-edged hillsides of scrap, Mr Buckminster organized metals according to type – heaps of copper, aluminium, and iron," says Purcell. "The rest of his inventory fell

RIGHT Rusted, worn, and patinated metal provides a backdrop for Purcell's assortment of found objects, all of which have been transformed through exposure to the outdoors. Among them are an anchor chain, a pile of copper floats from lavatory cisterns, and an array of decomposing books.

ABOVE A collection of "ruined" objects is displayed on plain shelving in Purcell's studio. Some are natural, some man-made; all have been "compromised" by being left outdoors in Mr Buckminster's junkyard.

RIGHT Purcell made these towers from found objects, mostly light fittings and pieces of old plumbing.

into ill-sorted miscellany and near-hopeless confusion. I built my collection by hunting through these piles of animal, vegetable, and mineral; in the studio, my finds constitute an abridgement of Buckminster's abridgement of the natural world."

Purcell makes "constructions" from her finds, either as installations or to be the subjects of her ambiguous and complex photography. The fact that their exposure outdoors has rid them of any sense of their former purpose or even their original nature is what she most relishes. "It means that they can be either repositioned as fictional elements in a new exhibition or used as a substitute for other well-known shapes, or simply have a metaphorical resonance that they did not originally possess." The studio/collection is not only a source for other work, but an artwork in itself. Purcell explains that she uses

groups of objects as metaphorical chunks in an imaginary, yet cohesive collection of pseudo-historical artefacts. In 2003 she recreated her studio as half of an exhibition called "Two Rooms": the other room was a recreation of the collection of curiosities owned by Danish physician Olaus Worm, based on an engraving of 1655. The juxtaposition emphasized the evolution of attitudes to collecting over three and a half centuries: while Worm's aim was to categorize the distinctions between animal, vegetable, and mineral, Purcell deliberately blurs these categories – she is keen to emphasize the transformations that can take place in the world around us. Unlike Worm, she is not interested in defining, but in the indefinite. "When you see an object that you are familiar with in everyday life so transformed it really takes you by surprise. That's what keeps me collecting."

ABOVE Weathered objects take on an elemental beauty when seen close-up. The miniature street lamp on the left is from a child's train set, while the pineapple-like sphere on a mount is actually a copper float from a lavatory cistern.

NEXT PAGE One wall of Purcell's studio/collection is composed of pieces of scrap metal, worn, rusted, and marked so that they take on the tones of an Old Master painting. In front are cases of disintegrating books, decayed pieces of furniture, and other battered objects.

"I have always suffered from a sickness that could be called the squirrel syndrome."

Arman, New York, NY, USA
AFRICAN ART

When Arman was a child, he had more toy soldiers than any of his friends. He also loved to categorize and re-categorize them, and to swap them continually in order to improve his collection. He comes from a long line of collectors, and acknowledges his obsession to be a family trait. "I have never been able to keep myself from collecting things," he says. "Everything that falls into my hands, from plants to stamps to seashells, primitive art, and even modern paintings, books, everything – I conceive of it as a whole. I have always suffered from a sickness that could be called the squirrel syndrome."

Arman collects – or has collected, for he quite regularly divests himself of entire collections in order to fund a new purchase – oceanic and aboriginal objects, vintage cars, cameras, pens, knives, guns, watches, Japanese arms and armour, jukeboxes, coloured radio sets from the 1950s, Tiffany lamps, perfume bottles, and 20th-century and contemporary art. His most important collection by far, however, is of African art, concentrating mostly on carved-wood figures and masks from Western and Central Africa, dating roughly from 1870 to the present day. It is a collection which numbers more than 400 objects, several of them masterpieces, and which is undoubtedly one of the best in the world. He is also extremely knowledgeable, making it his business to collect information as much as the objects themselves. He has garnered his knowledge by studying with top dealers, by close observation and, particularly, by handling the objects. "If you're not in constant confrontation with the material, you cannot become expert," he explains.

An all-or-nothing sense has characterized Arman's collecting for decades. The African collection, for example, was inspired by chance visits to two exhibitions in the 1950s that made a huge impression on him. Not long afterwards he began to buy, starting with a Dan mask from a flea market in Nice. Gradually, collecting grew in importance for him, consuming more and more of his time, efforts, and energy. Between 1975 and 1980 he was practically in a frenzy. He visited more or less every important exhibition, gallery, auction, and private collection, met regularly with dealers, museum directors, and other collectors,

RIGHT Since childhood, Arman has not been able to resist the lure of collecting. The idea of putting things of the same type together is similar to that of his work, in which accumulations feature similar objects crammed randomly into glass boxes. The displays at his New York apartment, however, are far from random, being beautiful and considered.

and would jump on a plane at a moment's notice to pursue a possible acquisition. He was even prevented from moving house when he spent the money intended for a new property on an ornate headrest from the Luba tribe. Eventually, in 1981, he felt he had to make the choice between his hobby and his profession. For four years he stopped going to exhibitions, and collected nothing.

Arman has never been a man to do things by halves. At the age of eight he learnt to play chess and devoted himself to improving his ability by reading books on the game. He has a black belt in judo and is expert in kung fu, is semi-professional at the Japanese board game Go, is a keen scuba diver, plays a mean game of ping pong, and is passionate about boxing and opera. He has studied Zen Buddhism and

astrology, mastered eight or nine foreign languages, and tries to play the piano.

And then, of course, there is his work. Arman is a world-famous artist, a founder of the New Realist School (whose interest was in new ways of seeing and thinking about life and art; roughly the equivalent of American Pop Art) and one of France's most talented avant-garde sculptors. Born Armand Fernandez in Nice in 1928, he studied philosophy and then art in Nice, and moved to Paris in 1949 to study Archaeology and Oriental Art at the Ecole du Louvre. Having first worked in the Surrealist and abstract styles, he later began to create "happenings", often collaborating with his friend and judo partner Yves Klein. In 1959, he began a series of works that he called "accumulations" – collections of similar objects

crammed randomly into boxes. He also began to create "poubelles", found garbage displayed in glass vit-
rines, and "destructions", works in which he
smashed, sliced, burnt, or otherwise destroyed objects
such as musical instruments, furniture, sculptural
reproductions, and manufactured goods. By this time
he was known, thanks to a printer's error in a catalogue, simply as Arman. Key themes of accumulation
and destruction have continued throughout Arman's
illustrious career, but typically he has never been nar-
row-minded about his work. Working from studios in
Paris and New York, he has also designed clothing,
jewellery, perfume bottles, and a racing car, written
and illustrated a children's book, designed the set for
an opera, and created a number of large-scale works
intended for public display and participation.

Clearly, the idea of accumulation runs
through Arman's life, both professionally and
personally. His collections, he says, follow the idea
of puttings things of the same type together, "which
is mine in many of my works, too". More complex
than that, however, is his need to challenge
preconceptions and explore our ideas about art,
everyday objects, and life itself, something which
he has done both at work and at play. Looking
at his Japanese armour and African sculptures, he
says: "What we see here is the anxiety and
hope that comes from trying to find a link with
the cosmos. Man is really the same everywhere,
seeking security and solutions. He asks the same
questions: 'What are we? Where have we come
from? Where are we going?'"

ABOVE **Arman, an
accumulator** *par excellence,*
celebrates the allure of
objects both in his work and
in his collecting. He loves
his coloured radio sets from
the 1950s, which are made
from a marbled plastic
called catalin.

"We realized that what we had been collecting had a name to it and that there was a niche."

Ruth & Marvin Sackner, Miami, FL, USA
CONCRETE POETRY

oncrete poetry, the artistic expression of written language, may seem like an acutely modern phenomenon, but it has its roots in pre-medieval times. There are examples in Chinese shaman books, Burmese lotus bud writings, Tibetan charms, Urdu amulets, Ethiopian magic texts, Arabic, Persian, and Armenian prayers, Turkish zodiacs, Hebrew amulets and prayers, Massoretic texts, Greek magical papyrus, and Latin prayers. Such writings, often mystical or sacred, have evolved over centuries and their contemporary forms are many and varied. They might include, for example, typewriter art, experimental calligraphy, correspondence and stamp art, sound and performance poetry, micrography, graphic design, poetic manuscripts and books, artists' books, and conventional poetry and prose written by concrete poets and visual artists.

Ruth and Marvin Sacker are interested in all of the above, though their collection focuses, due to lack of availability, less on the early work and more on pieces that date from around the time of Stéphane Mallarmé's seminal concrete poem "Un Coup de Dés" of 1897 and after. Theirs is an enormous and unrivalled archive of word and image art, containing more than 65,000 works, all stored and displayed in their home in Miami.

The Sackners have a fairly simple remit. Whereas most collectors aim for the finest examples that money can buy, they collect any relevant examples that they can afford. They collect work by around 200 artists from all over the world in great depth, in some cases buying almost everything the artist produces or has produced, and they collect other works relating to word and image art and poetry. "We decided to gather all works relating to concrete and visual poetry that we could afford to buy, irrespective of personal aesthetic considerations, along with their historic antecedents," explains Marvin Sackner. "We wanted to build a comprehensive, permanent collection that would not be altered by our personal biases."

The archive was established in 1979, but it was not the Sackners' first venture into collecting. Marvin Sacker had always had an interest in fine art, though he never dreamed that he would one day be able to afford to buy it. However, in a successful career as a pulmonary physician, during which time he became chief of medicine at Mount Sinai Hospital in Miami Beach, he invented a

RIGHT The large painting in the background is by the Sackners' friend and most valued artist, Tom Phillips. It reads: "The Marvin and Ruth Sackner Archive of Concrete and Visual Poetry".

ABOVE The gallery space within the Sackners' Miami home. *Walk Talk* is a piece printed on linoleum by German architect Fernaud Kriwet. When the Sackners visited his home they admired it, and he took a pair of scissors and chopped off a length to give to them.

medical device that began to bring him in some unexpected royalties. "It was like play money," he says. "I started to use it to collect contemporary art that we liked, and then of course the costs started to go above the income from the royalties – but by then it was too late." In the mid 1970s, the Sackners became interested in the Russian Avant Garde, and started to collect their work, though without a great deal of focus. Then in 1974 they happened to attend a show where they saw the work of Tom Phillips, a British word-image artist, and they were blown away by the idea that you could both read a work of art and look at the image at one and the same time. They went back the next day and saw the show again, and decided that they had to buy some of Phillips' work. They already had a few paintings which featured

words, not to mention the concrete/visual poetic sensibilities of their Russian pieces, and they added a few works in which word and image were related.

Not long afterwards, they were in a New York book store and fate led them to an anthology of concrete poetry by Emmett Williams. "We realized that what we had been collecting had a name to it," says Marvin. "And we recognized that we would never really have a great collection of Russian Avant Garde art, but that this art was available and not all that expensive. We also realized that there was a niche in the market, and that a global, international, and historical perspective seemed to be lacking in museums and private collections.

"We began our collection by making purchases from bookshops, art galleries, poets, and

artists. We bought Emmett's collection from him six months after reading his book. Purchases from bookseller catalogues soon followed. As we became more knowledgeable, we read exhibition and book reviews and made contact with dealers, artists, and poets for slides and photographs of their work for potential purchase. As our interests became known, we also received solicitations from such sources through the mail. Then we discovered the power of search engines and specialized websites on the Internet.

And so they have continued to collect, though not quite at the same pace as when they first started. They have also fostered close relationships with many of the artists, especially Tom Phillips, whose work was among the first pieces they bought. They acquired his original pages of *A Humument*, a book made by altering a Victorian novel, four or five years after falling in love with it at Basle, and it is still their favourite piece, added to on a regular basis as Phillips develops new imagery and poetry on pages of other copies of the book. The archive is particularly strong on work by historical movements of the 20th century – including the Russian Avant Garde, Italian Futurism, Dada, Surrealism, De Stijl, and French Lettrisme – on the experimental poets of the 1930s and '40s, and on concrete and visual poetry from the 1950s onwards. The Sackners are collectors, curators, cataloguers, correspondants and, occasionally, tour guides for the collection, which is displayed with meticulous and loving care around their house. "As we say when we get back from a trip," says Marvin Sackner, "it's home sweet museum."

ABOVE In the guest bedroom, rows of plan chests with slim drawers contain prints and drawings. On top, to the right, is a small, dark cabinet called *Museum of Ben*, a work by the French artist Ben Vautier.

NEXT PAGE The Sackners' eloquent dining room contains many more examples of word and image art. To stop people stumbling on the marble step, they have placed a length of sticky tape, bought at London's Tate Gallery, by Gilbert and George, which has the simple message: "Life Hope".

INDEX

Photographic acknowledgments

All photographs are by Deidi von Schaewen with the exception of the following.

1 Norwich Castle Museum and Art Gallery; 6 Bridgeman Art Library/Hamburg Kunsthalle, Germany; 8 Bridgeman Art Library/Ashmolean Museum, Oxford; 11 Uppsala Universitet, photo Mats Landlin; 13–14 Bridgeman Art Library/Prado, Madrid; 16 The Royal Collection © 2004, Her Majesty Queen Elizabeth II; 18–19 Heritage House Group Ltd; 21 Bridgeman Art Library/Towneley Hall Art Gallery and Museum; 22 Corbis/Massimo Listri; 25 RMN/Jean Schormans.